Melody of India Cuisine

Melody of India Cuisine

*Tasteful New Vegetarian Recipes
Celebrating Soy and Tofu
in Traditional Indian Foods*

By Laxmi Jain and Manoj Jain, M.D.

Woodbridge Press
Santa Barbara, California

Published and distributed by

Woodbridge Press Publishing Company
Post Office Box 6189
Santa Barbara, California 93160

Distributed simultaneously in Canada
Printed and bound in the United States of America

Library of Congress Cataloging-in-Publication Data:

Cover illustration: Janice Blair

Sketches throughout text: Kashmira Vora
Calculations of nutritional values, Nutritionist III software.

Library of Congress Cataloging-in-Publication Data

Jain, Laxmi.
  Melody of India cuisine : tasteful new vegetarian recipes
  celebrating soy and tofu in traditional Indian foods / by Laxmi Jain
  and Manoj Jain.
       p.   cm.
  Includes index.
  ISBN 0-88007-195-8 : $14.95
  1. Vegetarian cookery.   2. Cookery, Indic.   3. Cookery (Soybeans)
  I. Jain, Manoj.   II. Title.
  TX837.J16   1992
  641.6'334—dc20   92-7573
                                                             CIP

Acknowledgments

THIS BOOK is the fruition of the love, support and encouragement of our family and friends.

My husband, son, daughters-in-law, parents-in-law, Nandlal and Sajanbai Soni, parents Pannalal and Bhuribai Pandya, Moolchand Pandya, and Pushpa Pandya, all have contributed to the crumb and morsel of these recipes.

Special thanks go to Mr. N. N. Jain of Prestige Foods and Mr. Howard Weeks of Woodbridge Press for bringing our dream to life.

Laxmi Jain

*Dedicated to the poor and homeless
in India, Boston and throughout the world.*

Manoj Jain

Contents

Why Tofu and Soybeans?   15

In the Far East soybean has been harvested since ancient times. Only recently have Americans discovered soybean's merits. Only tofu and other soy foods can boast of providing a high-protein, low saturated fat and a cholesterol-free diet. This outstanding nutritional content can be combined with the traditional Indian cuisine to create exotic menus.

Nutritional Value of Tofu and Other Soy Foods   17

Soybeans provide the highest protein content of any plant food. Tofu maintains this high protein content with a low calorie content. Soy milk and soy yogurt are equally nutritious and well suited for lactose-intolerant individuals. These foods are ideal for vegetarians who want to maintain a high-protein diet and others who want a substitute for meat.

Preparation of Tofu and Other Soy Foods   21

Soy foods can be easily prepared at home. You soak the soybeans overnight, then blend the soaked soybeans and strain to make soy milk. The residue is soy okra, which is nutritious and high in fiber. Tofu is now widely available in most grocery stores. Simply put, soy foods are the golden path to a healthier and nourishing diet.

Soy Appetizers   33

Soy With Vegetables   63

Curried Vegetables

Stuffed Vegetables

Soy Desserts 171

Soy Ice Cream, Cookies and Cakes 193

Ice Cream

Soy Cookies

Cakes

Appendixes 211

Biographical Notes 221

Introduction

MOM AND I started dabbling on our book twelve years ago on a modest 1960 Underwood typewriter, the same typewriter my Dad had used to type his Ph.D. thesis. Frequently, in the morning with my lunch, Mom would hand me several recipes to correct as I would head out to school. Mom was a traditional Indian cook, and I was a student of nutrition and medicine. A complementary relationship developed and in time, the Underwood gave way to an IBM PC and the scattered recipes took shape into this unique cookbook.

Mom is well known for her culinary skills in our extended family and in the community. Among her experiments in cooking she stumbled upon tofu. With each tofu recipe she realized the many potentials of soybean. Meanwhile, I was skeptical of soy. "It's probably some weird-tasting food which scientists feed their laboratory rats." None of the nutrition literature or books by Shurtleff and Akiko could change my mind.

It wasn't until Mom disclosed her secret. All the great-tasting dishes which she was preparing were made from soy. She was adding 20 percent soy flour to the chappati (bread) to double its protein content and using tofu instead of milk curd, paneer, to lower the cholesterol content in our food. I was so impressed that I joined Mom full force in promoting soy.

My formal research on soy began through a Medical Perspective Grant. I took my mother's newly found secret for a pilot test. Near our home town in India, soy was being grown as a cash crop for oil and not used as a food product. With affiliation from local organizations I conducted training programs in 10 villages on the high nutritional value, low cost and easy preparability of soybean. The villagers were amazed by the soy milk, soy yogurt and tofu. We felt we had uncovered a secret treasure.

In the chapters ahead the merits of soy are discussed, yet as a physician I cannot stress enough the advantages of a soy-based vegetarian diet over animal products. The reduction in coronary artery disease (the leading cause of mortality in the United States) and colon cancer can be credited to a low cholesterol and high fiber diet.

This book is not just about soybean but also about vegetarianism. To us, vegetarianism entails not only sound nutrition but also a deep sense of spirituality. Vegetarianism is a manifestation of our belief in *ahimsa*, which means non-violence. This is the same non-violence which Gandhi and Martin Luther King used to obtain freedom and racial equality. By being a vegetarian one brings ethics and spirituality into daily practice. One makes a statement, "I shall not harm any living beings, shall they be humans or animals."

A vegetarian diet is healthful, moral and economical. It is surely destined to be the diet of the future generations, with soybean as a major protein source.

We sincerely hope this book helps you in striving toward your goal of a healthier and more fulfilling life, just as it has for our family and friends.

Manoj Jain
April, 1992

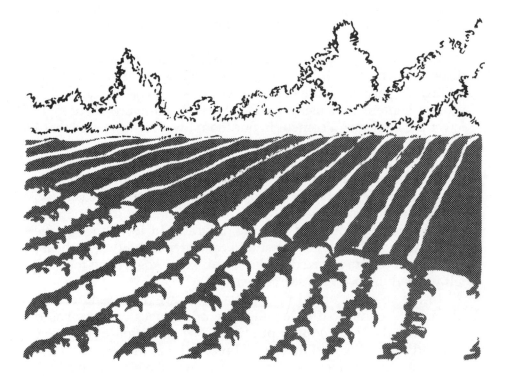

CHAPTER 1

Why Tofu and Soybeans?

SOYBEANS HAVE BECOME a hallmark of a highly nutritious diet. They are far superior to other beans and to meat products because of their high-protein, low saturated fat, and cholesterol-free content. Soybeans are very versatile and can be made into soy milk, tofu, soy yogurt, miso, and tempeh. With so many varieties of soy foods offering such good nutrition, you only need recipes to introduce soybeans into your diet.

Soy foods have customarily been considered "bland and taste-less." And it's true, raw tofu tastes like dough. But just as dough can be baked into a delicious loaf of bread, tofu and other soy foods can come alive in a variety of dishes. You can achieve this exotic taste, texture, and color in soy foods by combining them with "the spices of India."

Spices transform soy's simple taste into a tantalizing cuisine. Tofu, when soaked in curry or mixed with spiced vegetables, absorbs the rich taste in its every pore, becoming a delectable meal. A simple lettuce and cucumber salad turns into a raging high-protein, low-calorie tofu salad. Plain soy milk becomes a fragrant saffron milk with cardamom and almonds. Chappati, bread made from whole wheat, is doubled in its protein content when made partially from soy flour. The possibilities are endless.

This book introduces and explores the innovative concept of soy seasoned with spices. Specifically, it caters to three different inter-ests. First, it is an opportunity for those interested in learning Indian cooking. A tremendous synergistic effect occurs when soy-beans are incorporated into Indian cuisine, something never done before! Over 150 recipes presented here are the result of careful testing and tasting. Second, for those who thought that the plain taste of soy food outweighed its health benefits, this book dually guarantees a savory and a healthful meal. Last, it is for those who are vegetarians or just want to reduce their meat intake and yet maintain a high-protein diet. This book is a must for all who are interested in a soybean diet, Indian cuisine, or vegetarian cooking.

The second and third chapters describe the nutritional aspects of soybeans and how the basic soy foods, such as tofu and soy milk, can be made in your own home. The book also introduces simple strategies of Indian cooking. If you have hesitated to learn Indian cooking because you thought it was too difficult, too time consuming, or just beyond your reach, you can conquer your fear through this book. Once you comprehend the basic concepts, they will no longer be intimidating, and you can confidently prepare Indian food and even experiment with your own recipes.

The book is devoted to recipes following the introductory chapters. These recipes have been created and tested to incorporate soybeans into Indian cuisine. Comparative nutritive values of the recipes are given to reveal the health benefits of a soybean diet. The sections are divided into soy appetizers, soy vegetables, soy breads, soy salads, soy raitas and chutney, soy rice and lentils, soy drinks and soy sweets. There is a tremendous variety capable of suiting any and all tastes.

This book will open up new culinary horizons providing a golden opportunity to increase your repertoire of nutritious recipes.

Table 1: Comparison of protein, fat and carbohydrate content in common vegetarian foods.

Nutritive Values of Common Foods

Name 100 Gm.	Protein Gm.	Fat Gm.	Carbohydrate Gm.
Rice (raw, milled)	6.8	0.5	78.2
Wheat Flour (whole)	12.1	1.7	69.4
Almonds	20.8	58.9	10.5
Cashew nuts	21.2	46.9	22.3
Coconut (fresh)	4.4	41.6	13.0
Peanuts	25.3	40.1	26.1
Milk, Cow's	3.2	4.1	4.4
Lentils	25.1	0.7	59.0
SOYBEANS	**43.2**	**19.5**	**29.4**

CHAPTER 2

Nutritional Value of Tofu and Other Soy Foods

SOYBEANS ARE rightly praised for their nutritive qualities. Of all the plant products on this earth, they have the highest protein content. Soybeans are 40 percent protein, 35 percent carbohydrate, 20 percent fat and the remaining 5 percent minerals. Their nutritive value compared with other foods is shown in Table 1.

The 40 percent protein content of soybeans is extremely beneficial to the vegetarian diet. Protein is important for the repair and growth of the body, especially muscles, blood, brain and heart, and is essential for growing children. If there is protein deficiency in the diet, the child will be stunted in his mental and physical development. Just 100 to 120 grams of soy is ample to provide a growing child with the adequate amount of protein. The child would need to eat twice as many lentils to get the same amount of protein. In addition, soybean protein has all eight essential amino acids that our bodies need. No other plant protein can meet these criteria.

Carbohydrates provide some of the energy needed for our body to function. This energy can be in the form of sugar, which is instantly utilized, or starch which is slowly digested. In diseases such as diabetes a high sugar content is unhealthy, and patients must limit their carbohydrate intake. Soybeans are low in carbohydrates and high in protein and fiber content, hence ideal for diabetic patients. Tofu, for example, has one of the lowest calorie-to-protein ratios.

Table 2: Comparison of nutrition in 100 grams of milk (in percent)

Nutritive Values of Milk

	Soy Milk	Cow's Milk	Breast Milk
Water	88.6	88.6	88.6
Protein	4.4	2.9	1.4
Calories	52	59	62
Fat	2.5	3.3	3.1
Carbohydrate	3.8	4.5	7.2
Calcium mg.	18.5	100	35
Phosphorus	2.5	36	15
Iron mg.	1.5	0.1	0.20

Source: Standard Tables of Food Composition (Japan)

Fat is the most concentrated source of energy in the diet. The fat from soybeans can be extracted in the form of soy oil. The quality of soy oil surpasses that of other oils in that it has the two essential fatty acids (linoleic and linolenic) required by the body. It is very high in polyunsaturates and contains no cholesterol. In contrast, meat and animal shortenings, such as lard, contain saturated fats which elevate blood serum cholesterol, linked to heart disease and hypertension.

Soybeans contain important minerals such as lecithin, which interacts with bile to reduce free-floating cholesterol in the bloodstream, hence again reducing the risk of heart disease. Although an enzyme called trypsin inhibitor is found in raw soybeans, inhibiting the absorption of protein in the body, it is easily and quickly destroyed by the heat of cooking. Soybeans are especially rich in calcium, which is essential for bone development and growth, and iron, which is necessary for red blood cell formation.

This high quality of nutrition in soybeans is found in most of their products, such as soy milk, tofu, and soy yogurt. Table 2 compares soy milk with cow's milk and breast milk. Soy milk is high in protein and iron. Soy milk is an excellent alternative for children who have lactase deficiency and cannot digest cow's milk. Furthermore, in many individuals the ability to digest lactose (milk sugar) decreases as they get older, resulting in gas cramps and indigestion after drinking cow's milk. Soy milk provides better nutrition and causes no indigestion.

The nutritional value of soy foods can best be appreciated when the basic soy foods are incorporated in our regular diet. A study done by scientists showed that when soybeans were added to Indian foods such as chappati or dal the protein content increased tremendously. The comparative values of soybean and non-soybean food are shown in Table 3.

Table 3: The nutritive value of traditional recipes with and without soybean supplements.

Nutritive Value of Various Recipes

Recipes	Amount per Serving	Protein gm.	Fat gm.	Carbohydrate gm.	Calories
Chappati (20% soy flour)	4 Chappaties 100 gm.	18.40	5.26	59.70	358
Chappati (No soy flour)	4 Chappaties	11.80	1.50	71.2	346
Salad (soy)	100 gm.	11.0	4.8	9.85	211.5
Salad (no soy)	100 gm.	1.8	—	7.45	206.0
Cutlets (soy potato patties)	2 cutlets (68 gm.)	11.60	5.11	11.4	137
Cutlets (no soy)	2 cutlets (68 gm.)	1.21	2.15	12.8	54
Chikki (soy sweet)	100 gm.	21.80	9.80	57.95	407
Chikki (ground nut sweet)	100 gm.	13.40	20.4	60.8	475

Source: Walker et al., JNKVV Research Journal, Vol. 11, No. 1 and 2, 1977.

Without a doubt, soybeans are an ideal food for vegetarians. The high protein content allays the fears of a protein-deficient diet among new vegetarians.

So in conclusion, soybeans are high in both quality and quantity of protein, contain no cholesterol, no saturated fat, have a low calorie-to-protein ratio and are the ideal food for vegetarians, heart disease patients and those on a special diet. The nutritional contents of soy are almost too good to be true, and it makes one wonder, "Why have soybeans not been used much until now?" The answer is simple. Basic soy foods such as soy milk, soy flour, tofu, or indigenous soy recipes were never introduced to many parts of the world, including India—that is, until now. The following chapters provide you with all the know-how of Indian soy cuisine. Your new knowledge will be bound to impress family and friends.

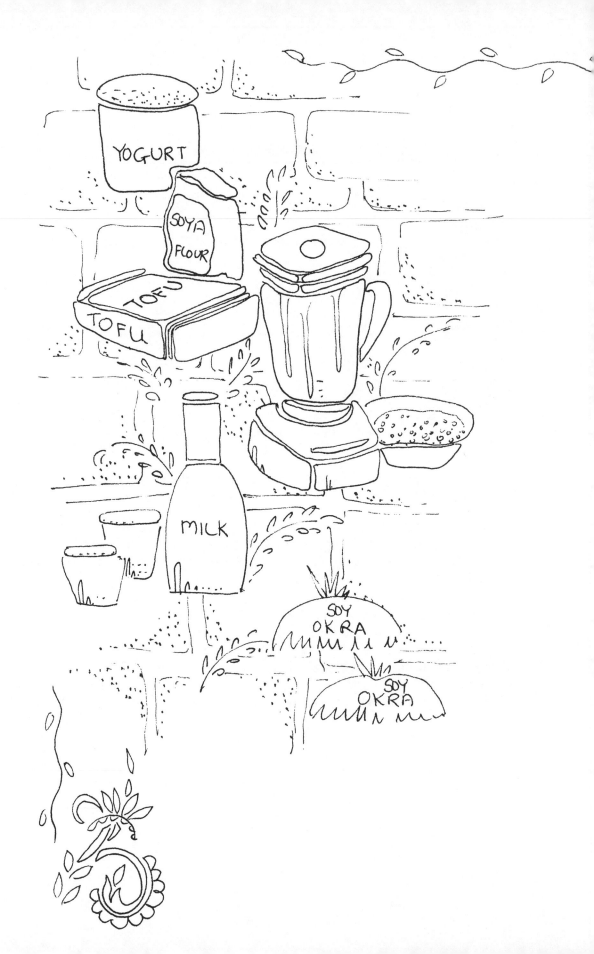

CHAPTER 3

Preparation of Tofu and Other Soy Foods

A WONDERFUL QUALITY of the soybean is that it is universally versatile. It can be used in everything from soy sauce to soft soaps, from curds to cookies, and from paints to pastry. Though the industrial and chemical uses of soy are innumerable, our interest lies in its edible uses.

Over 150 recipes, all derived from several basic soy foods, are presented here. The basic soy foods are soy flour, soy lentils, soy paste (soaked and blended soybeans), soy okra, soy milk, soy yogurt, and tofu. Though you can buy most of these at the store, it is easy to make your own soy milk, soy yogurt or tofu at home. The following are basic methods for the preparation of soy flour, soy milk, soy paste, soy yogurt, soy okra and tofu.

Soy Flour

Soy flour can be bought commercially or made at home by simply grinding dry soybeans. It is lighter and fluffier than wheat flour and has a creamy yellow color with a nut-like flavor. There are two kinds of soy flour, full fat and low fat. The former contains 40 to 45 percent protein, 20 percent fat, and is high in calories, while the latter has a higher amount of digestible protein and only 1 to 7 percent of the fat. Soy flour is the richest source of protein in the diet when compared with other food products such as beans, cheese, steak, pork, eggs, peanut butter, etc. It contains a high amount of vitamin B complex, calcium, potassium, phosphorous, lecithin and iron. The nutrition content in the recipes is calculated from full fat soy flour. Defatted soy flour can be substituted for full fat soy flour in most recipes for a low fat diet.

One of the simplest uses of soy flour is to mix it with whole-wheat flour in the proportion of 1:4 when making breads such as chappati or parathas. This simple strategy boosts the protein content from 11.8 grams of protein to 18.3 grams in a 100 gram chappati. This addition of soy flour does not alter the taste, texture or appearance of whole-wheat chappati. Similarly, in other recipes where wheat flour is used, soy flour is a quick and easy additive. In other dishes soy flour can replace chick-pea flour, converting a low-protein food into a high-protein, delightful meal.

Whole Dry Soybeans

Whole dry soybeans can be used in traditional as well as everyday dishes replacing kidney beans, chick-peas, or dried lima beans. This adds a new flavor and a nutritious change to the recipe.

Soaking soybeans

Place dry soybeans in cold water 3 to 4 times their volume. Soak the beans for at least 6 to 8 hours, until fully expanded in the water. A good time to soak them is overnight. It is best to refrigerate the soaking beans, otherwise they may sour and produce an unpleasant taste. Also be sure to drain and resoak the beans 2 to 3 times in a day to keep them fresh.

If time is limited you can shorten the soaking time by another method. Add beans to boiling water and continue to boil for 2 minutes. Then set the beans aside for an hour or more before proceeding with cooking. The boiling ruptures the hard shells of the beans so they swell more quickly.

Cooking soybeans

To cook soybeans, cover the pot and allow them to simmer over low heat for about one hour. There is no need to stir soybeans during the cooking. You may check them occasionally to make sure they have not absorbed all the water. If they have, add hot water and just cover them again. When cooking soybeans, ½ teaspoon of baking soda for every pound of beans can be added. This will make the soybeans soft.

Total cooking and soaking time can be reduced to 55 minutes if a pressure cooker is used, and the beans will have a wonderful texture and delicious flavor. Wash 1 cup of dry soybeans. Place beans in a 6-quart pressure cooker with 2 cups of cold tap water. Close lid and set pressure regulator. Cook for 15 minutes after first whistle; then remove cooker from heat and wait until the pressure drops. When you are sure it has dropped, remove the lid and drain the beans.

Soy Lentils (Soy Dal)

Soy dal is soaked, dehulled and split soybeans and is similar to lentils in appearance. It is an asset in the repertoire of recipe ingredients because it mixes with and replaces other lentils while doubling the protein content and adding a nutty flavor. Many enjoyable recipes are presented in the soy with rice and lentils section.

Preparing soy lentils

There are three methods for splitting and hulling whole soybeans and making soy lentils.

1. Clean and soak soybeans overnight or for 6 to 8 hours. In the morning wash them again. Split and dehull the soybeans by squeezing them with a kneading motion, a handful at a time. Wash and drain the soybeans and discard the hulls as they float to the surface. Repeat several times until all soybeans are split and dehulled.

2. Clean and soak soybeans overnight or for 6 to 8 hours. In the morning wash them again and boil them for 20 minutes. When soybeans are cool, split and dehull the soybeans by squeezing them with a kneading motion, a handful at a time. Wash and drain the soybeans and discard the hulls as they float to the surface. Repeat several times until all soybeans are split and dehulled. Boiling the soybeans makes splitting and dehulling easier and faster.

3. Clean dry soybeans of any impurities. Place a handful of soybeans in a blender, set the "chop" selector, and chop until each soybean is split into 2 to 4 pieces. Place the split soybeans on a plate and separate the hulls from the soybeans. Similarly chop and dehull all the soybeans and store in a tightly covered container. When a recipe calls for soy dal just soak the chopped soybeans overnight or for 6 to 8 hours.

Soy Milk

There are several methods for making soy milk at home. It can be made either from soy paste or from soy flour. Both methods are described below, however the soy milk from the paste generally comes out better.

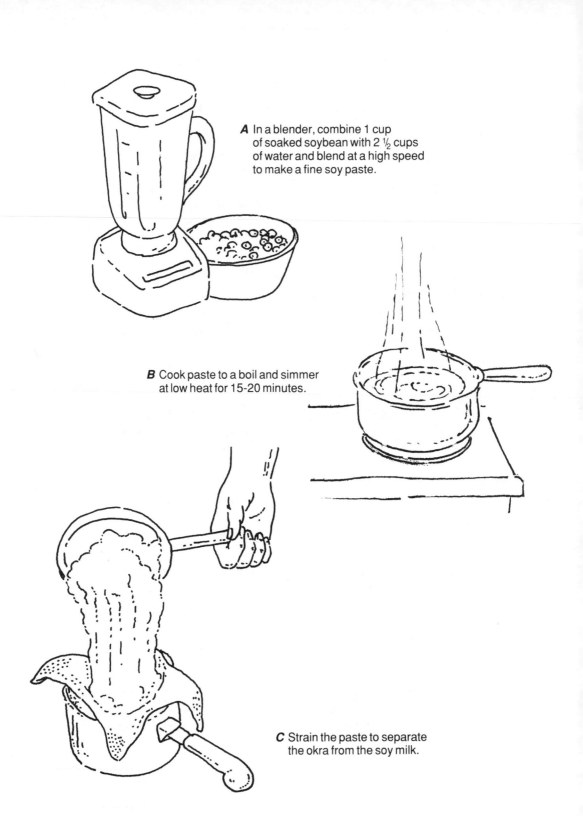

A In a blender, combine 1 cup of soaked soybean with 2 ½ cups of water and blend at a high speed to make a fine soy paste.

B Cook paste to a boil and simmer at low heat for 15-20 minutes.

C Strain the paste to separate the okra from the soy milk.

Soy Milk

Soaking the soybeans:

1. Rinse 2 cups whole soybeans and soak them overnight in 5 to 6 cups of hot water. Next morning, rinse again 3 to 4 times in a colander.

2. For quick soaking, rinse the beans and then pour boiling water on them and allow them to soak for about 3 to 4 hours, or until beans are double in size.

Grinding the soybeans

3. In a blender combine 1 cup soaked soybeans and 2½ cups of water. Blend the beans at high speed to a fine soy paste. The soy paste can be used for other recipes.

Cooking the soy milk

4. Place the soy paste in a double boiler or in a heavy pot that does not burn easily.

5. Cook the soy paste on medium-high heat and bring to a boil, stirring constantly to prevent scorching.

6. When the soy milk starts to boil, turn down the heat and simmer on low heat for about 15 to 20 minutes.

Straining the soy milk:

7. Set a piece of thin cheesecloth over a big pot. Pour the hot soy milk into the cloth.

8. All the milk will strain into the pot below. Twist the cloth tightly and press the bag with a wooden spoon to extract all the milk.

9. Set aside the pulp that remains in the cloth. This pulp is called "soy okra." You can use it for other recipes.

10. The soy okra can be stored in the refrigerator for 3 to 4 days. It can also be dried in sunlight and stored for use at a later time as stuffing.

METHOD 2: SOY MILK FROM SOY FLOUR

Soy milk can also be made from soy flour. This saves the trouble of soaking and grinding the soybeans.

1. In a heavy pan mix 1 cup of soy flour and 4 cups of water. To prevent lumps mix slowly. Let it stand 1 to 2 hours.

2. Use a heavy pan and cook on medium heat about 40 to 50 minutes. Keep stirring to prevent scorching and foaming.

3. Strain through a sieve or cheesecloth. Add more water if the soy milk is thick.

The soy milk made at home has a light yellow color and a distinct beany flavor. In China and Japan this is well-liked; however, in the beginning it may be difficult for you to become accustomed to this taste. Fortunately, now-a-days you can purchase commercial soy milk without the beany taste, if desired.

There are many advantages to using soy milk, the high nutritive quality being by far the most important. Soy milk has high protein and low fat, qualities which are highly recommended by doctors.

Soy Paste

Soaked and blended soybeans form soy paste. It is an intermediate product in the process of making soy milk. This paste can be thin or thick depending on how much you blend it and how much water you add. Unless specified otherwise, it is best to keep it thick. The paste will have a beany aroma, which disappears when it is combined with other ingredients in a recipe.

Many dishes are made from soy paste. Soy chillas are thin spicy soybean pancakes and make a delightful appetizer. The sweet dish, soy halva, can be made from soy paste. Though it requires some effort to make, it is a great dessert favorite. The taste is delectable, and the nutritional quality is superb.

A special delight for South Indians who enjoy coconut chutney is soy chutney, another dish made from soy paste. It is identical in taste and appearance to coconut chutney, yet more nutritious.

Soy Yogurt

It may be puzzling at first to discover that milk can be made from a bean, yet it's even more surprising to discover that yogurt can also be made from the same beans.

Soy yogurt can be made like cow's milk yogurt. You can make yogurt from pure soy milk or from a mixture of soy milk and cow's milk.

Method:

1. Heat the soy milk to a boil, then allow it to cool until warm; pour the milk into a clean pot.

2. Add 1 tablespoon yogurt starter for every 2 cups of milk. Use only plain cow's milk yogurt (not soy yogurt starter).

3. Stir the yogurt starter into the soy milk, cover it, and keep it in a warm place for 4 to 6 hours.

4. If the yogurt separates easily from the pot sides when you tilt the pot gently, it's done. Keep it in the refrigerator.

For a thick yogurt, make thick soy milk and add a little more yogurt starter.

Soy yogurt can be mixed with vegetables to make raitas, adding variety and nutrition to the meal. Prepared soy yogurt is starting to be marketed in America and has a great deal of potential as a health food.

Soy Okra

After straining soy milk, the fibrous residue that remains is called soy okra. In appearance this resembles mashed potatoes and is a good source of fiber. Soy okra is low in calories, but still contains 17 percent of the original soybean protein. Soy okra can be used for stuffing in various vegetable dishes.

The nutritional content of one cup wet soy okra is compared with oatmeal. See Table 4.

	Soy okra	Oatmeal
Fiber	5.42	0.5
Calories	156	148
Carbohydrate (gm.)	16	26
Protein (gm.)	8.3	5.4

Tofu

Tofu is made from soy milk. For making the tofu you need:

1 cup dry soybeans
4 to 5 cups water
¼ cup of lemon juice

1. First make thick soy milk, as described above. After the soy milk is strained, boil it on slow heat, stir slowly in a circular motion, and pour in half of the lemon juice. Slowly stir in opposite direction.

2. Pour a small amount of the remaining lemon juice over the top of the soy milk. Cover the pot to retain the heat for proper curdling and set aside for 5 minutes.

3. The tofu will start to form large white curds. If the soy milk is still milky, add a little more lemon juice, and cook on low heat.

4. When done, large white pieces of tofu will be floating in a clear yellow liquid called whey.

5. If the whey is cloudy, not all the milk has coagulated, and less tofu will be made. This is possible if not enough lemon juice was added, or if it was added too fast, or if the beans were not ground fine enough.

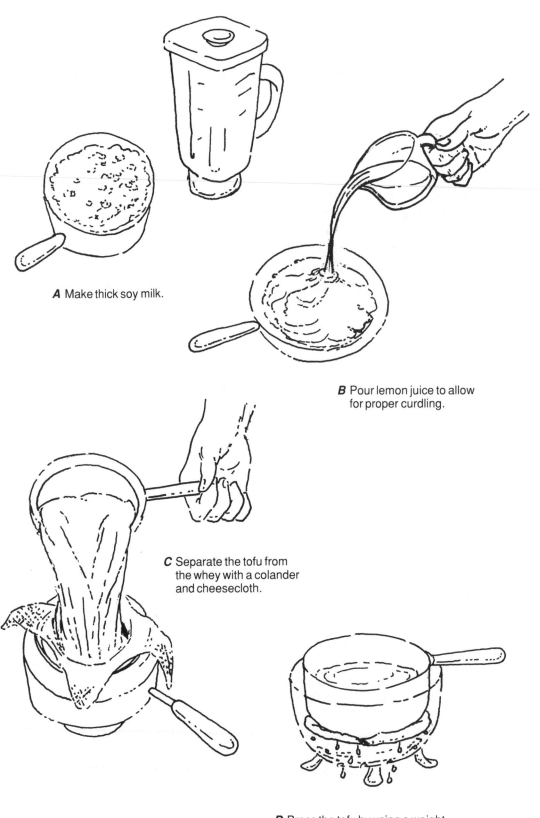

A Make thick soy milk.

B Pour lemon juice to allow for proper curdling.

C Separate the tofu from the whey with a colander and cheesecloth.

D Press the tofu by using a weight such as a pan of water.

Tofu

Pressing the tofu

1. Set a colander in the sink and cover with a thin cloth, like a cheesecloth. Pour all the tofu into the cloth.

2. To press the tofu use a heavy weight. A jar of water or a clean heavy rock or brick can be used for pressing. Keep tofu pressed for 20 to 30 minutes.

3. Remove the weight. Tofu should be firm to the touch. Store it in a container of cold water in the refrigerator. Change the water daily to help preserve freshness. If stored properly, it can be kept up to a week.

Tofu is also called bean curd. It is almost identical to "paneer." If you are familiar with Indian cooking, you may know that paneer is milk curd and is a delicacy made on special occasions.

The quality and texture of tofu varies greatly. There are soft, medium, and hard tofus; the difference is due to the percentage of water in the tofu. The recipes in the book are geared for medium tofu, yet you can substitute your favorite.

The advantages of tofu are enormous. It's good nutrition and can be prepared in various ways. The freshness of salad greens mixed together with pieces of tofu make a delightful combination. By adding tofu pieces to vegetables, you can savor the dish in a variety of possibilities. The tofu absorbs the spicy taste and aroma of the sauces. Numerous sweet dishes such as sweet carrot cake can also be made from tofu.

As you can see, the potential of soybeans is boundless. Once you realize the amazing advantages, including the delicious taste, of using soybeans in your meals, you will never turn back! Not only will you have increased your repertoire in Indian recipes, but you will have a diet high in protein and low in cholesterol, and you will be loving every minute of it.

Melody of India
Recipes

Soy Appetizers

JUST AS A GOOD PREVIEW has the moviegoers rushing to the theater, a good appetizer has the diners tantalized in anticipation of the upcoming meal. An attractive, tasty appetizer is a guaranteed topic of conversation. Soy appetizers are no exception.

Roasted soybeans, soy crunchies (soy mathari), soy flour spicy crunchies (namkin shakerpara) are all appealing appetizers. They are light, so they do not fill you up before a meal, and go well with drinks. These appetizers are simple dishes and can be quickly pulled from the shelf when an unexpected guest arrives for afternoon tea.

Tofu samosas (pastry stuffed with tofu and potatoes), and kachori (deep-fried pastry stuffed with soybeans), are extravagant appetizers. Often their irresistible taste persuades guests to have extra helpings. It is best to serve only one or two pastries to avoid overtaxing the palate. Many of these appetizers are deep-fried, which adds to the fat content of the foods. For a healthier and low fat diet the fried foods should be wiped with a paper napkin which will soak the residual oil.

Soy idli (steamed soybean cake), soy dosa (soybean and rice pancake) or soybean chilla (thin soybean pancake) are often substituted for a meal, especially for a simple light evening dinner. Soy flour and chick-pea flour provide the necessary nutrition and protein for a good meal.

Some cool appetizers for a summer garden party are khaman dhokla (a spicy soy cake), and dahi baras (soybean and mung dal patties in yogurt). The white yogurt's simple taste contrasts with the deep, dark-colored and tartar taste of the tamarind chutney. It is sure to tantalize the palate for the meal.

Pakoras, which are fritters, are presented in several varieties. Vegetable pakoras, soybean and mung dal pakoras, and aloo and tofu pakoras (potato fritters with peanuts and tofu) are exotic-tasting and nutritious appetizers.

Soy appetizers are sure to delight and impress your guests.

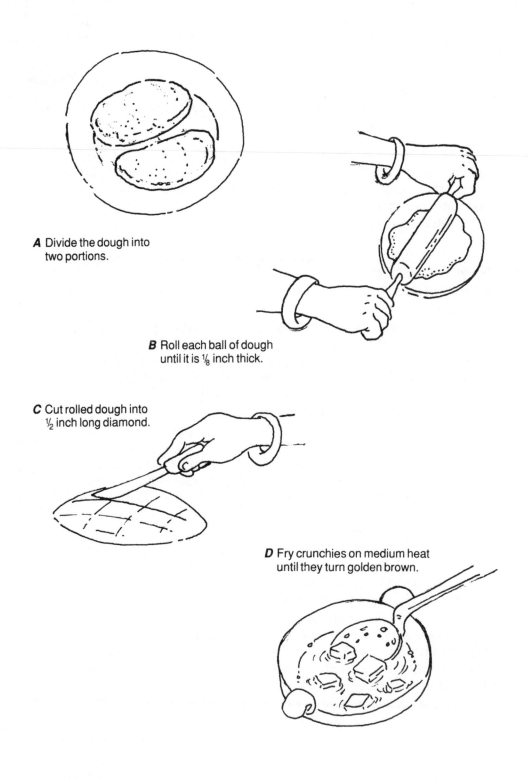

A Divide the dough into two portions.

B Roll each ball of dough until it is ⅛ inch thick.

C Cut rolled dough into ½ inch long diamond.

D Fry crunchies on medium heat until they turn golden brown.

Soy Crunches

Soy Crunchies
Soy Mathari

Soy matharis are a versatile snack. They go well with milk at breakfast, replace cookies in the lunch box, are perfect with afternoon tea, or make a nutritious midnight snack.

2 cups all-purpose flour
¾ cup soy flour or defatted soy flour
⅓ cup soy oil
1 teaspoon ajwain seeds
1 teaspoon salt
soy oil for deep-frying
about ½ cup water

1. Combine all-purpose flour, soy flour, salt, ajwain seeds, and ⅓ cup oil in a bowl. Adding a little water at a time, make a stiff dough. Divide the dough in half and form 2 balls.

2. Roll each ball until it is about ⅛ inch thick. If it sticks while rolling, sprinkle with dry flour or use a little oil. Cut into ½ inch diamond shapes or stick shapes.

3. Heat the soy oil in a deep frying pan. Fry the mathari in oil on medium heat until golden brown. Remove with a slotted spoon and place on a paper towel. Wipe with another paper towel to soak up the residual oil.

4. Serve warm or cold as snacks.

Servings: 10   Time: 30 min.

Nutritional analysis per serving:

Calories	197	(RDA% 10)
Protein	6 gm	(RDA% 14)
Carbohydrate	22 gm	
Fat	12 gm	

Soy Flour Spicy Crunchies

Soy Namkin Shakerpara

Like mathari, shakerpara can be used in a variety of ways. On our last camping trip to Vermont, we enjoyed shakerpara all along the scenic drive.

1 cup whole-wheat flour
½ cup soy flour or defatted soy flour
½ cup chick-pea flour
2 teaspoons chili powder (according to taste)
2 teaspoons salt (according to taste)
½ teaspoon turmeric powder
1 teaspoon cumin seeds
2 teaspoons fennel seeds
½ teaspoon ajwain seeds
¼ cup soy oil
½ cup water
pinch of asafetida
soy oil for deep-frying

1. Combine all the ingredients except the oil for deep-frying. Add water a little at a time and make a stiff dough. Divide the dough in half and form 2 balls.
2. Roll each ball until it is about ⅛ inch thick. If it sticks while rolling, sprinkle with dry flour or use a little oil. Cut into ½ inch long diamond shapes.
3. Heat soy oil in a deep frying pan. Fry namkin shakerpara in oil on medium heat until they turn golden brown, about 10 to 12 minutes. Remove them with a slotted spoon and place on a paper towel. Wipe with another paper towel to soak up the residual oil.
4. Serve warm or cold any time with tea or coffee.

Servings: 6   Time: 40 min.

Nutritional analysis per serving:

Calories	292	(RDA% 15)
Protein	7 gm	(RDA% 16)
Carbohydrate	23 gm	
Fat	19 gm	

Roasted Soybeans

Roasted soybeans are hearty snacks for growing youngsters.

¾ cup soybeans
1 teaspoon salt (according to taste)
½ teaspoon chili powder (according to taste)
½ teaspoon ground cumin seeds
½ teaspoon cream of tartar
2 teaspoons soy oil

1. Soak soybeans overnight or for 6 to 8 hours.
2. Wash and drain the soybeans and put them on a baking sheet. Bake at 350 F for 20 to 30 minutes until they turn golden brown.
3. Sprinkle with salt, pepper, cream of tartar and soy oil. Mix well and let cool before serving.

Servings: 6   Time: 30 min.

Nutritional analysis per serving:

Calories	138	(RDA% 7)
Protein	12 gm	(RDA% 28)
Carbohydrate	6 gm	
Fat	7 gm	

A Make a soft dough.

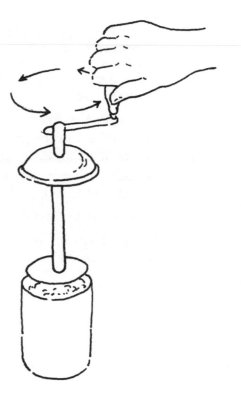

B Fill greased saive machine with dough.

C Turn machine over hot oil to make saive.

Saive

Savory Soy Flour Noodles

Saive

Once you start eating saive you can't put away the bowl. My husband and son finish off a week's supply in just a few sittings.

2 cups chick-pea flour
1 cup soy flour
3 teaspoons salt (according to taste)
2 teaspoons chili powder (according to taste)
1 teaspoon ajwain powder (optional)
1 teaspoon cumin seed powder (optional)
½ teaspoon clove powder (optional)
¾ cup water
⅓ cup soy oil
pinch of asafetida
soy oil for deep-frying

1. Mix all the ingredients (except water and oil for deep-frying) in a bowl. Add enough water to make a soft dough. Beat by hand for 4 to 5 minutes.
2. Put the dough in a greased saive machine.
3. Heat soy oil in a deep frying pan. Make the saive over the oil by turning the machine. Fry for ½ to 1 minute.
4. Take the saive out and drain on a paper towel. Serve warm or cool. Store in an air-tight container.

Note: This recipe requires a saive machine. This can be purchased at Indian stores.

Servings: 8   Time: 40 min.

Nutritional analysis per serving:

Calories	289	(RDA% 14)
Protein	11 gm	(RDA% 24)
Carbohydrate	21 gm	
Fat	18 gm	

Savory Vegetable Fritters

Vegetable Pakoras

In India, during the monsoon rains, pakoras are the popular appetizers. Made from freshly harvested vegetables or lentils, they are a nutritious beginning to a meal.

1 cup soy flour or defatted soy flour
1 cup chick-pea flour
1½ cups water
1½ teaspoons chili powder (according to taste)
3 teaspoons salt (according to taste)
2 teaspoons fennel seeds
1 teaspoon cumin seeds
½ teaspoon garam masala
2 tablespoons chopped green chilies
3 tablespoons chopped green coriander leaves
pinch of asafetida
soy oil for deep-frying
10 potato slices, 10 cucumber slices, 10 spinach leaves, and 10 green chilies.

1. In a bowl combine soy flour, chick-pea flour and spices. Add water to make a thick batter.

2. Heat soy oil in a deep frying pan. Take one slice of vegetable at a time, dip in the batter, and put them one by one in the oil. Fry a few pakoras at a time in the hot oil.

3. Fry for a few minutes and then stir occasionally until they are golden brown.

4. Serve warm with tomato, mint or coriander chutney.

This recipe can also be used with cauliflower, eggplant or zucchini slices.

Servings: 4   Time: 35 min.

Nutritional analysis per serving:

Calories	340	(RDA% 17)
Protein	17 gm	(RDA% 37)
Carbohydrate	33 gm	
Fat	17 gm	

Soybean and Mung Fritters

Soybean and Mung Dal Pakoras

½ cup soybeans
½ cup mung lentils
¼ cup chick-pea flour
2½ teaspoons salt (according to taste)
1½ teaspoons chili powder (according to taste)
1 teaspoon cumin seeds
1 teaspoon coriander seeds (optional)
2 teaspoons fennel seeds
1 teaspoon garam masala
1 tablespoon chopped ginger
1 tablespoon chopped green pepper
3 tablespoons chopped coriander leaves
pinch of asafetida
soy oil for deep-frying
½ cup water

1. Soak soybeans and mung lentils overnight or for 6 to 8 hours. Wash and drain, then blend into a paste by adding water.
2. Mix dal paste with all other ingredients except oil for frying.
3. Heat soy oil in a fry pan until it is very hot. Take 1 teaspoon of the batter at a time and drop in the hot oil. Fry a few pakoras at a time in the hot oil.
4. Fry for a few minutes and then stir occasionally until golden brown.
5. Serve warm with tomato, mint or coriander chutney.

Servings: 8   Time: 40 min.

Nutritional analysis per serving:

Calories	182	(RDA% 9)
Protein	10 gm	(RDA% 23)
Carbohydrate	13 gm	
Fat	10 gm	

Potato Balls

With Peanuts and Tofu

Aloo Bada

Aloo badas are traditionally dipped in sweet and sour chutney, but my children enjoy them with ketchup.

1½ cups mashed tofu
4 cups potatoes, boiled, peeled, and mashed
½ cup chopped peanuts
¼ cup raisins
1 teaspoon chili powder (according to taste)
3 teaspoons salt (according to taste)
2 teaspoons fennel seeds
3 tablespoons chopped coriander leaves
3 tablespoons lemon juice
3 tablespoons chopped green pepper
1 tablespoon chopped ginger
1 teaspoon garam masala
soy oil for deep-frying

For batter

1 cup chick-pea flour
1 teaspoon salt
½ cup water

1. Mix all the ingredients except oil. Make 25 to 30 equal balls out of the potato mixture. Apply oil to hands to prevent mixture from sticking.
2. Combine chick-pea flour, salt and water in a bowl and mix well. In a frying pan heat soy oil. Dip the potato balls one at a time into the batter and drop 4 to 5 balls at a time in the hot oil. Turn and fry on medium heat until balls become brown.
3. Serve hot with chutney or ketchup.

Servings: 6   Time: 50 min.

Nutritional analysis per serving:

Calories	348	(RDA% 17)
Protein	11 gm	(RDA% 24)
Carbohydrate	41 gm	
Fat	18 gm	

Potato Patties

With Tofu

Aloo Tofu Ticci

Aloo tofu ticci is a hearty snack that can also be a light meal when served with chick-peas and sweet chutney.

3 cups boiled and mashed potatoes
1 cup mashed tofu
1 teaspoon chili powder (according to taste)
2 teaspoons salt (according to taste)
2 teaspoons chopped green chilies
3 tablespoons chopped coriander leaves
2 teaspoons chopped ginger
soy oil for frying

1. Mix all the ingredients, except soy oil. Make 20 to 24 patties, about 2 inches in diameter. Apply oil to hands to prevent mixture from sticking.

2. Heat a flat frying pan over low heat and spread one tablespoon oil in it. Put as many patties as possible in the pan. Fry patties on low heat until the bottoms turn a nice brownish color.

3. Turn the patties over and cook the other side in the same way. Add a little more oil for the next batch and fry all the patties in this way. Serve hot with chutney.

Servings: 4   Time: 40 min.

Nutritional analysis per serving:

Calories	181	(RDA% 9)
Protein	4 gm	(RDA% 9)
Carbohydrate	19 gm	
Fat	10 gm	

Pastry
Stuffed with Tofu and Potatoes
Tofu Samosas

Walking through the bazaar in India, you cannot miss the road-side vendors, surrounded by folks of all ages enjoying the spicy samosas or kachoris accompanied by chutney or ketchup.

For dough

2 cups all-purpose flour
1 teaspoon salt
4 tablespoons soy oil
soy oil for deep-frying
about ½ cup water

For filling

1 cup mashed tofu
2 cups potatoes, boiled and cut into small pieces
1 cup boiled green peas
2 teaspoons chili powder (according to taste)
2 teaspoons salt (according to taste)
½ teaspoon turmeric powder
2 teaspoons fennel seeds
½ teaspoon cumin seeds
½ teaspoon garam masala
1 teaspoon mango powder
2 teaspoons chopped green chilies
3 tablespoons chopped green coriander leaves
2 teaspoons chopped ginger
¼ cup soy oil
pinch of asafetida

1. For filling, heat ¼ cup of soy oil in a large pan. Add cumin seeds and asafetida, and fry for a few seconds. Add tofu and fry for 1 minute. Add remaining ingredients, and mix thoroughly. Cover and cook on low heat for about 5 minutes, then set aside to cool.

2. In a bowl, mix flour, salt and 4 tablespoons oil. Add a little water at a time and make a stiff dough. Cover and set aside for 20 minutes, then knead for 5 minutes.

3. Divide dough into 12 equal balls. Roll balls into thin circles, about 3 to 4 inches in diameter. If too sticky, add some flour.

4. Cut each circle in half. Take the half-circle and make a cone by moistening the edges with water to seal. Hold the cone in one hand between the index finger and thumb.

5. Fill the cone with about 1 to 1½ tablespoons of potato filling. Moisten edges at top of the cone and seal carefully to form a triangle. Make all the samosas in the same way.

6. Heat oil in a frying pan. Fry samosas on medium heat until golden brown. Serve hot with chutney or ketchup.

Servings: 8   Time: 90 min.

Nutritional analysis per serving:

Calories	363	(RDA% 18)
Protein	7 gm	(RDA% 15)
Carbohydrate	36 gm	
Fat	22 gm	

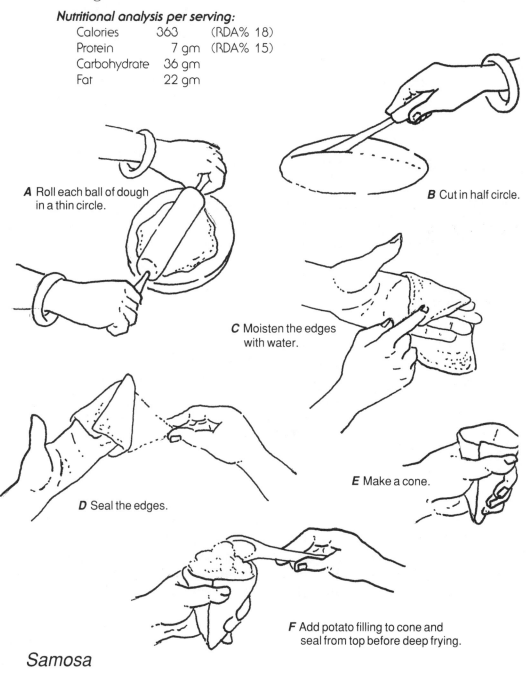

A Roll each ball of dough in a thin circle.

B Cut in half circle.

C Moisten the edges with water.

D Seal the edges.

E Make a cone.

F Add potato filling to cone and seal from top before deep frying.

Samosa

Deep-Fried Pastry
Stuffed with Soybeans
Kachori

For dough

3 cups all-purpose flour
1 teaspoon salt
⅓ cup soy oil
1 cup water
soy oil for deep-frying

For filling

½ cup mung dal
⅓ cup soybean
2 teaspoons salt (according to taste)
2 teaspoons chili powder (according to taste)
¼ teaspoon turmeric powder
½ teaspoon garam masala
2 teaspoons fennel seeds
1 tablespoon chopped green chilies
½ tablespoon chopped ginger
2 tablespoons chopped coriander leaves
4 tablespoons soy oil
½ teaspoon cumin seeds
pinch of asafetida

1. Wash the mung dal and soybeans and soak overnight or for 6 to 7 hours. Wash and coarsely grind to a thick paste.

2. In a bowl mix flour, salt and soy oil. Add a little water at a time and make a dough. Cover and set aside for 30 to 40 minutes. Knead for 10 minutes and make 20 to 22 balls. Apply oil to hands to prevent dough from sticking. Cover the dough and set aside for 8 to 10 minutes.

3. In a heavy frying pan heat 4 tablespoons of oil. Add cumin seeds and asafetida; fry for a few seconds. Add the paste to the frying pan. Fry for 30 minutes on low heat or until paste becomes slightly golden. Add all the ingredients for the filling and mix properly. Make 20 to 22 small balls.

4. Take one ball of dough at a time and form it into a cup and fill with a soy ball. Gather up edges and press by hand to form a round flat kachori, or roll it lightly.

5. In a deep frying pan heat soy oil until it starts smoking. Reduce heat to low and fry the kachoris a few at a time. It will take about 20 to 25 minutes to make them crisp and brown. When brown, remove from oil and drain. Serve with chutney.

Servings: 8   Time: 180 min.

Nutritional analysis per serving:

Calories	416	(RDA% 21)
Protein	12 gm	(RDA% 27)
Carbohydrate	43 gm	
Fat	22 gm	

A Form the dough into cups and fill each with one soy ball.

Kachori

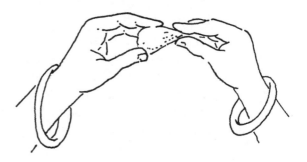

B Gather edges to form kachori before deep frying in soy oil.

Deep-Fried Pastry

Stuffed with Tofu and Green Peas

Matar Kachori

For dough

>3½ cups all-purpose flour
>½ cup soy oil
>1 teaspoon salt
>1¼ cup water
>soy oil for deep-frying

For filling

>4 cups shelled green peas
>1 cup tofu
>4 teaspoons salt (according to taste)
>3 teaspoons chili powder (according to taste)
>1 teaspoon garam masala
>3 teaspoons fennel seeds
>2 tablespoons chopped green chilies
>1 tablespoon chopped ginger
>4 tablespoons chopped coriander leaves
>4 tablespoons soy oil
>½ teaspoon cumin seeds
>pinch of asafetida

1. In a bowl mix flour, salt and soy oil. Add a little water at a time and make a dough. Cover and set aside for 30 to 40 minutes. Knead for 10 minutes and make 30 balls out of the dough. If it sticks apply oil to hands. Cover and set aside for 10 minutes.

2. Pick over and wash the peas well and coarsely grind into a thick paste. In a heavy frying pan heat 4 tablespoons of oil. Add cumin seeds and asafetida and fry for a few seconds.

3. Add the paste and mashed tofu to the pan. Fry for 30 minutes on medium heat or until paste becomes thick and cooked. Add all the filling ingredients and mix well. Make into 30 small balls.

4. Take one flour ball in your palm and form it into the shape of a cup. Fill it with one ball of peas. Gather up the edges of flour ball and press by hand to form a round flat kachori.

5. In a deep frying pan heat soy oil unti it starts smoking. Reduce heat to low and fry the kachoris a few at a time. It will take about 20 to 25 minutes to make them crisp and brown. When brown, remove from the oil and drain. Serve with chutney.

Servings: 8   Time: 180 min.

Nutritional analysis per serving:

Calories	495	(RDA% 25)
Protein	11 gm	(RDA% 25)
Carbohydrate	50 gm	
Fat	28 gm	

Soybean Patties

In Yogurt

Dahi Baras

A delight for dieters, dahi baras are patties dipped in yogurt and topped with sweet and tangy tamarind chutney. They combine good taste, good looks and good nutrition.

1 cup mung lentils
½ cup soy lentils or soybeans
2 tablespoons salt
about 1 cup water

For the yogurt

3 cups plain yogurt or low fat yogurt
2 tablespoons sugar
1 teaspoon salt

For decoration

1 cup tamarind chutney
½ cup mint chutney
1 teaspoon salt
1 teaspoon chili powder (according to taste)
2 teaspoons roasted cumin seeds
3 tablespoons green coriander leaves

1. Soak the soy lentils or soybeans and mung lentils overnight or for 6 to 8 hours. Drain and blend into a fine paste by adding 1 cup water. Beat the paste for 5 minutes.

2. In a heavy frying pan heat the soy oil. Make baras (patties) with the help of a serving spoon. Drop one serving spoonful of paste in the oil for each bara.

3. Drop as many baras into the oil as the frying pan can hold at one time. Fry them for 2 to 3 minutes, or until they are golden brown. Make all the baras in the same way.

4. Have ready a large bowl of hot water, and add 2 tablespoons salt. When baras are fried, take them out with a slotted spoon and place them in the hot water. Let them soak for 30 to 40 minutes.

5. When baras become soft, remove from water. Place one bara at a time on your palm and squeeze it gently with the other hand. Do the same thing for all the baras. Arrange them on a large serving plate.

6. Put the yogurt in a bowl and beat lightly until it is smooth and creamy. Add sugar and salt and pour over the baras.

7. Spread the tamarind and mint chutney over the dahi baras so as to partially cover the yogurt. Sprinkle all other garnishing ingredients evenly over the top. Serve dahi baras cold.

Servings: 8   Time: 50 min.

Nutritional analysis per serving:

Calories	219	(RDA% 11)
Protein	16 gm	(RDA% 36)
Carbohydrate	26 gm	
Fat	6 gm	

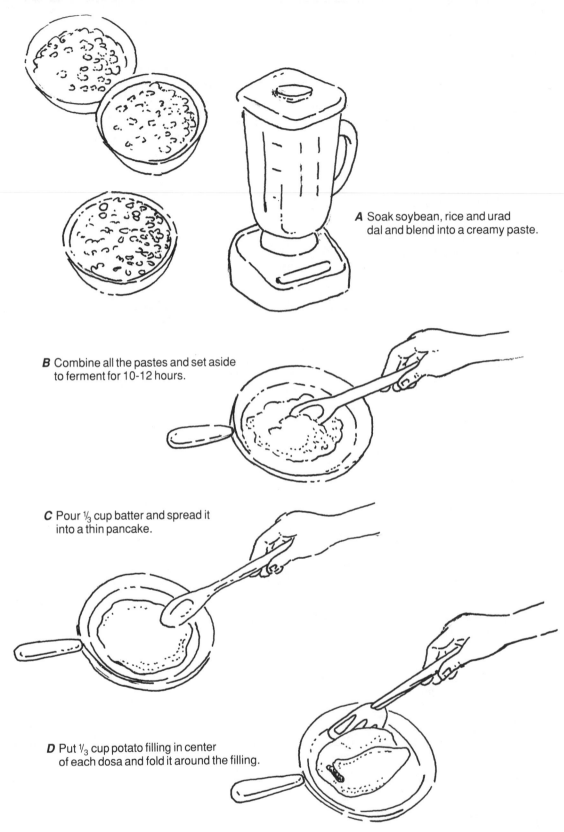

A Soak soybean, rice and urad dal and blend into a creamy paste.

B Combine all the pastes and set aside to ferment for 10-12 hours.

C Pour ⅓ cup batter and spread it into a thin pancake.

D Put ⅓ cup potato filling in center of each dosa and fold it around the filling.

Dosa

Soybean and Rice Pancakes
Soy Dosa

Though my family was raised in North India, they enjoy South Indian dishes such as soy idli and soy dosa. Soy dosa is like a crepe with potato filling. It serves as a lunch or a light dinner.

½ cup soybeans
½ cup urad dal (split black gram lentils without skin)
3 cups rice
2 teaspoons salt
soy oil for frying
about 4 to 5 cups water

Potato filling for dosa

10 cups boiled and chopped potatoes
¼ cup soy oil
2 large onions chopped (optional)
1 tablespoon chopped ginger
3 tablespoons chopped green chilies
1 teaspoon mustard seeds
½ teaspoon ground turmeric powder
2 teaspoons coriander powder
3 teaspoons chili powder (according to taste)
4 teaspoons salt (according to taste)
5 tablespoons lemon juice
5 tablespoons cashew nuts (optional)
5 tablespoons chopped coriander leaves
pinch of asafetida

1. Wash soybeans, urad dal and rice in separate bowls. Cover with cold water and let them soak overnight or for 6 to 8 hours.

2. Blend dal, rice and soybeans by adding a little water until they become creamy. Combine all the pastas, water and salt. Cover and set aside at room temperature for at least 10 to 12 hours to ferment.

3. In a heavy skillet, heat one teaspoon of oil over medium heat. Pour ⅓ cup batter and spread it in the shape of a very thin pancake with the back of a spoon or a rubber spatula. Spread batter as thin as possible for a crisp dosa. Spread a little oil around the edges. Cook for 2 to 3 minutes, turn it over with a wide metal spatula and cook the other side for a minute or two or until it's golden brown. If it is sticky put a little oil around the edges.

4. Prepare filling by heating soy oil. Fry mustard seeds for a few seconds, then add chopped onions and fry until they become brown. Add cashew nuts and fry for a few seconds. Add all other ingredients for filling, mix well for another 2 to 3 minutes. Put ⅓ cup of potato filling in each dosa, roll it around the filling, and serve warm with coconut chutney.

Servings: 6   Time: 60 min.

Nutritional analysis per serving:

Calories	392	(RDA% 20)
Protein	11 gm	(RDA% 24)
Carbohydrate	64 gm	
Fat	10 gm	

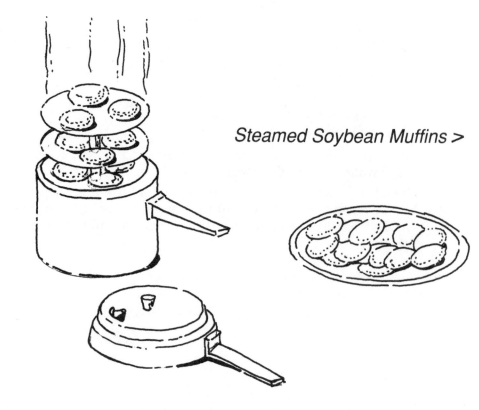

Steamed Soybean Muffins >

Steamed Soybean Muffins

Soy Idli

For a Sunday brunch, idli is a good choice. Soy idli is a traditional South India dish made from rice, soy and lentils. It is steamed in the pressure cooker, making it light and nutritious. Idli is an elegant brunch preparation when served with sambhar and soy chutney.

3½ cups uncooked rice
½ cup soybeans
⅓ cup urad dal (split black gram without skin)
2 teaspoons salt (according to taste)
about 1½ cups water

1. Wash and soak rice, dal and soybeans overnight in separate bowls. In the morning drain and grind each of them separately in the blender by adding a little water until they become thick and creamy. Mix all pastes in a large pan and add salt. Cover and set aside in a warm place for 7 to 8 hours until fermented. For best results, the batter should be fermented.

2. Grease the cups of an idli mold (or muffin tin), then place one large spoon of batter into each greased cup. Pour water into a large wide pan or pressure cooker. Place mold in the pressure cooker or pan and cover to steam; don't put pressure weight on the cooker. Cook the idli for 10 to 15 minutes. Remove from steam and wait for 2 minutes before removing from cups.

3. Serve warm with coconut chutney and soy sambhar.

Servings: 6 to 8   Time: 50 min.

Nutritional analysis per serving:

Calories	387	(RDA% 19)
Protein	14 gm	(RDA% 31)
Carbohydrate	73 gm	
Fat	3 gm	

Thin Soybean Pancakes
Soybean Chilla

Soybean chillas, spicy pancakes made from chick-pea or soy paste, are a delight on rainy afternoons. Chillas are best enjoyed with chutney or ketchup.

1½ cups mung lentils
½ cup soybeans or soy lentils
¼ cup chick-pea flour
2 teaspoons salt (according to taste)
3 teaspoons chili powder (according to taste)
1 teaspoon cumin seeds
2 teaspoons fennel seeds
1 teaspoon garam masala
2 teaspoons chopped ginger
2 tablespoons chopped green chilies
3 tablespoons chopped coriander leaves
soy oil for frying
3 to 4 cups water

1. Soak soybeans and mung dal overnight or for 6 to 8 hours. Wash and drain.
2. Blend soybeans and mung dal in a paste by adding water a little at a time. Mix with all the other ingredients, except oil for frying.
3. Heat a frying pan, preferably non-stick. Spread 1 teaspoon oil around the pan. Put ¼ cup of paste in the pan, and spread it out in a very thin pancake with the back of a spoon or a rubber spatula. Spread paste as thin as possible for a crisp pancake. If it is sticky put 1 teaspoon oil around the pancake.
4. Cook for 1 to 2 minutes on medium heat. Turn it with a wide spatula and cook the other side for 1 to 2 minutes, or until it turns golden brown. If it is sticky put a little oil around the edges.
5. Serve warm soybean pancake with chutney.

Servings: 6   Time: 60 min.

Nutritional analysis per serving:

Calories	371	(RDA% 19)
Protein	23 gm	(RDA% 52)
Carbohydrate	39 gm	
Fat	14 gm	

Thin Chick-Pea and Soy Flour Pancakes

Gram Flour Chilla

1 cup soy flour or defatted soy flour
1 cup chick-pea flour
2½ teaspoons chili powder (according to taste)
2½ teaspoons salt (according to taste)
2 teaspoons fennel seeds
1 teaspoon cumin seeds
½ teaspoon garam masala
2 teaspoons chopped green chilies
3 tablespoons chopped green coriander leaves
pinch of asafetida
soy oil for frying
2½ to 3 cups water

1. In a bowl combine flour and spices. Add water to make a thin paste.
2. Heat a non-stick frying pan. Spread 1 teaspoon oil around the pan. Put ¼ cup of the paste on the pan and spread it out in a very thin pancake with the back of a spoon or a rubber spatula. Spread paste as thin as possible for a crisp pancake.
3. Cook for 1 to 2 minutes, or until bubbles begin to form on the surface. Turn it over with a wide spatula and cook each side for 1 to 2 minutes or until it turns golden brown. If it is sticky put a little oil around the edges.
4. Serve warm chilla with chutney.

Servings: 4   Time: 50 min.

Nutritional analysis per serving:

Calories	304	(RDA% 15)
Protein	15 gm	(RDA% 35)
Carbohydrate	25 gm	
Fat	17 gm	

Soy Flour Rolls

Pitorh

For my daughters-in-law, pitorh is one of the challenging dishes to make. It requires talent to form the batter into smooth rolls. But when successful, the rolls taste wonderful and look appealing.

1¼ cup chick-pea flour
½ cup soy flour
3 cups water
1 teaspoon chili powder (according to taste)
1½ teaspoons salt (according to taste)
½ teaspoon turmeric powder
½ teaspoon cumin seed
pinch of asafetida

For decoration

1 tablespoon soy oil
1 teaspoon mustard seeds
3 tablespoons chopped coriander leaves
2 tablespoons grated fresh coconut
pinch of asafetida

1. Mix all ingredients well. Heat mixture, stirring constantly.
2. When mixture becomes very thick, simmer it on very low heat for 4 to 5 minutes. Test by spreading a little on a plate; if after 2 minutes the mixture can be rolled and lifted, it is ready for spreading.
3. When ready, spread the mixture thinly with the back of a large spoon on an oiled plate.
4. Cool for 4 to 5 minutes. Cut it into 1-inch strips. Roll up the strips and arrange on the plate.
5. In a small vessel heat the oil and fry the mustard seeds. When the seeds start popping, remove from the heat, add the asafetida and pour over the arranged rolls.
6. Garnish with chopped coriander leaves and grated coconut.

Note: A pitorh raita can be made by cutting pitorh in small square pieces and mixing them in yogurt.

Servings: 6   Time: 40 min.

Nutritional analysis per serving:

Calories	161	(RDA% 8)
Protein	9 gm	(RDA% 21)
Carbohydrate	21 gm	
Fat	5 gm	

Spicy Cake

With Mixed-Lentils

Handvo

Handvo and dhokla (see next recipe) are nutritious spicy cakes. They combine several types of lentils, which are high in protein and low in fat, into a delicious and aromatic preparation.

Handvo is baked and khaman dhokla is steamed. Each has a unique texture and taste.

¾ cup soybeans
2 cups rice
½ cup toovar dal (dried pigeon pea pulse)
¼ cup mung dal
¼ cup chana dal (split chick-pea lentils)
3 cups grated squash
1 cup sour yogurt
8 hot green chilies
2 tablespoons chopped ginger
½ cup soy oil
2 teaspoons lemon juice
4 teaspoons sugar
1 teaspoon soda
2 teaspoons chili powder (according to taste)
3 teaspoons salt (according to taste)
½ teaspoon turmeric powder
2 teaspoons mustard seeds
1 tablespoon sesame seeds
3 tablespoons chopped coriander leaves
pinch of asafetida
about 1 cup warm water

1. Wash and soak the soybeans, toovar dal, rice, mung dal and channa dal in plenty of water overnight or for 6 to 8 hours.
2. Wash and drain the soybeans, toovar dal, rice, mung dal and channa dal, then grind in a blender with the yogurt and hot water. Make into a thick paste.
3. Keep in a warm place to ferment for at least 5 hours.
4. Blend green chilies and ginger, then add 4 tablespoons of oil, asafetida, lemon juice, soda, sugar, chili powder, turmeric powder, salt, and grated squash (with the water squeezed out). Mix well.

5. Spread this batter in a greased baking tin. Heat remaining soy oil in a small vessel and add the mustard seeds when oil is heated. When mustard seeds pop up, add sesame seeds and asafetida. When sesame seeds turn brown, spread the oil and seeds all over the batter.

6. Bake in a hot oven at 400 F for 30 to 35 minutes or until the crust is brown.

7. Cut into pieces and garnish with chopped coriander leaves. Serve with hot pickles and chutney.

Servings: 8   Time: 60 min.

Nutritional analysis per serving:

Calories	453	(RDA% 23)
Protein	17 gm	(RDA% 38)
Carbohydrate	53 gm	
Fat	19 gm	

Spicy Soy Cake
Khaman Dhokla

1 cup chick-pea lentils
½ cup soy lentils or soybeans
1 cup yogurt
6 green hot chilies
2 tablespoons chopped ginger
4 tablespoons soy oil
2 teaspoons eno
2½ teaspoons salt
4 teaspoons lemon juice
about ½ cup hot water

For seasoning (tarka)

¼ cup soy oil
1 teaspoon mustard seeds
2 tablespoons fresh coconut
2 tablespoons sesame seeds
3 tablespoons chopped green coriander leaves
1 tablespoon chopped green chilies
pinch of asafetida

1. Wash and soak the chick-pea lentils and soybeans or soy dal in water overnight. The next morning, wash and drain the chick-pea lentils and soybeans, then grind in a mixer with green chilies, ginger, yogurt and hot water, to make a thick paste. Add 4 tablespoons soy oil and salt to the paste and keep in a warm place to ferment for at least 5 to 6 hours.

2. Boil water in a large pan or pressure cooker. Grease a 10-inch cake pan.

3. In a bowl place 2 teaspoons lemon juice, one teaspoon eno and half of the paste. Stir mixture quickly and thoroughly, and pour immediately into the greased pan. Steam without pressure for 15 to 20 minutes or until the khaman dhokla is done. Remove from steam and wait for 4 minutes or until it cools. Cut into squares.

4. Heat ¼ cup soy oil in a small pan, add mustard seeds and asafetida. Fry for a few seconds, add sesame seeds, coconut, and chopped green chilies, and fry for a few more seconds.

5. Garnish dhoklas with seasoning mixture and coriander leaves. Serve with green chutney.

Servings: 8   Time: 50 min.

Nutritional analysis per serving:

Calories	344	(RDA% 17)
Protein	19 gm	(RDA% 43)
Carbohydrate	31 gm	
Fat	16 gm	

Soy with Vegetables

ONE CAN DISTINGUISH Western recipe books from Eastern recipe books by the number of pages devoted to vegetables. In the West, vegetables are the most neglected foods, whereas in the East they form the "meat" of the diet.

In Indian cuisine vegetables have several basic preparation styles. They can be stuffed, made dry, or made with a sauce. The traditional stuffing is potatoes, which are high in carbohydrates, 22.6 percent, and low in protein, 1.6 percent. A tastier and healthier substitute is tofu which brags a low carbohydrate content of 2.4 percent and a high protein content of 9 percent. Also, soy okra and soy flour can serve as wonderful stuffings. The possibilities of recipes are innumerable. Combine your repertoire of favorite vegetables, about 20, with three choices of soy stuffings and you have 60 recipes at your fingertips. Our favorite dishes are stuffed tomatoes and stuffed bell peppers with tofu.

Other vegetable recipes can be dry or moist. A dry vegetable dish is spinach and fried tofu. Some saucy vegetable dishes are cabbage soy flour kofta curry and mixed vegetable korma with tofu. With vegetable dishes, the tofu absorbs the savory spicy flavor and the vegetable retains its individual splendid taste. The combination leads to a magnificent end product. Saucy curried vegetables are a wonderful combination with breads.

All these vegetable dishes will make you ask for a second helping. The vegetables are excellent sources of vitamin A and vitamin C, while tofu provides a high protein, low calorie supplement.

A Grate the cabbage.

B Squeeze the grated cabbage.

C Make balls from cabbage and kofta ingredients.

D Fry kofta until they turn brown.

Patta Gobha Kofta Curry

Cabbage and Soy Flour Balls Curry

Patta Gobhi Kofta Curry

Like eating a warm cake before it's frosted, my children finish off the cabbage soy balls (kofta) before the curry is made. This dish resembles meat balls in a sauce and is a common party preparation because of its ease and attractiveness.

For Kofta

2 cups grated cabbage
¾ cup soy flour
¼ cup chick-pea flour
2½ teaspoons salt (according to taste)
1 teaspoon chili powder (according to taste)
½ teaspoon turmeric powder
2 teaspoons chopped ginger
soy oil for deep-frying

Grind into a paste (for sauce)

2 large onions
3 large tomatoes
1 teaspoon chili powder (according to taste)
2 teaspoons coriander powder
2 teaspoons salt (according to taste)

For seasoning (tarka)

3 tablespoons soy oil
½ teaspoon cumin seeds
2 bay leaves
1 teaspoon coriander seeds
pinch of asafetida

For decoration

3 tablespoons chopped coriander leaves
½ teaspoon garam masala
1 tablespoon chopped green pepper

1. Squeeze the grated cabbage to extract moisture. Add all the kofta ingredients except oil. Mix well and form into 18 to 20 small balls.
2. Heat the soy oil in a heavy frying pan and fry a few balls at a time on medium-high heat. Fry them until they turn brown, then set aside.

3. Heat the soy oil in a wide frying pan and put all the seasonings in it. Fry for a few seconds then add sauce paste and cook for 7 to 8 minutes, or until oil starts oozing out.

4. Add 2 to 3 cups of water to the paste and boil it. Add koftas to the pan and sprinkle with garam masala. Bring to a boil once more and remove pan from heat. Garnish with chopped coriander leaves and chopped green pepper. Serve warm.

Servings: 8   Time: 50 min.

Nutritional analysis per serving:

Calories	154	(RDA% 8)
Protein	5 gm	(RDA% 12)
Carbohydrate	12 gm	
Fat	10 gm	

Peas and Tofu Curry >

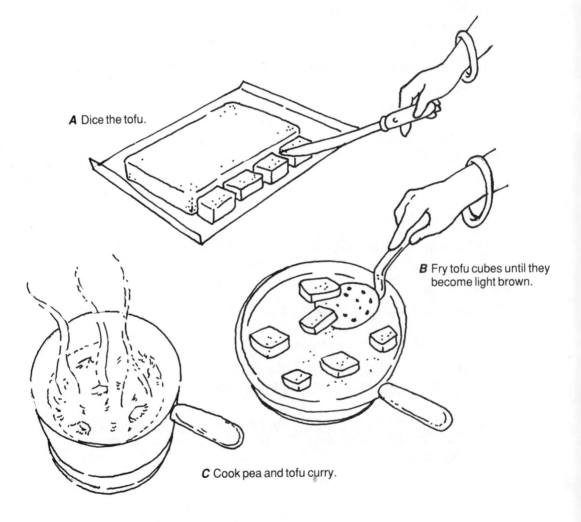

A Dice the tofu.

B Fry tofu cubes until they become light brown.

C Cook pea and tofu curry.

Pea and Tofu Curry
Matar Paneer

When we take a break from cooking and go out for Indian food, we have discovered matar paneer to be a favorite dish in Indian restaurants. The taste of sweet peas in a spicy curry sauce is enjoyed by most people.

2 cups shelled green peas
1 cup tofu, diced
4 tablespoons soy oil
½ teaspoon cumin seeds
1 bay leaf
½ teaspoon garam masala
4 tablespoons chopped coriander leaves
soy oil for deep-frying
pinch of asafetida
2 to 3 cups water

Grind into a paste (for sauce)

2 cups chopped tomatoes
1 cup chopped onion (optional)
1 teaspoon chili powder (according to taste)
1 teaspoon salt (according to taste)
½ teaspoon turmeric powder
2 teaspoons coriander powder
1 tablespoon chopped ginger root
1 green chili
1 tablespoon lemon juice

1. Deep-fry the tofu cubes in oil, until they become light brown. In a heavy pan heat 4 tablespoons of oil, and add cumin seeds, asafetida leaf and bay leaf. Fry for a few seconds, then add all the paste and cook until the paste starts oozing oil, about 8 to 10 minutes.
2. Add 2 to 3 cups of water and peas. Let cook until peas are tender. Add tofu paneer and let cook for 3 to 4 minutes. Sprinkle with garam masala.
3. Garnish with coriander leaves and serve warm.

Servings: 6   Time: 30 min.

Nutritional analysis per serving:

Calories	163	(RDA% 8)
Protein	6 gm	(RDA% 13)
Carbohydrate	12 gm	
Fat	11 gm	

Potato Curry

With Soy Yogurt

The art of making this potato curry is using the soy yogurt. The yogurt adds a slightly tangy and rich taste which goes perfectly with rice dishes.

3 cups potatoes, boiled and diced
½ cup plain yogurt
½ cup soy yogurt
1 teaspoon chili powder (according to taste)
2 teaspoons salt (according to taste)
½ teaspoon turmeric powder
½ teaspoon cumin seeds
1 teaspoon chopped ginger
2 tablespoons chopped coriander leaves
3 tablespoons soy oil
pinch of asafetida
1½ cups water
3 tablespoons lemon juice

1. In a bowl put potatoes, yogurt, chili, salt, turmeric powder, lemon juice and water. Mix well.

2. In a deep heavy frying pan heat the soy oil; add cumin seeds, ginger and asafetida. Fry them for a few seconds, add the potato-yogurt mixture and stir until the yogurt comes to a boil.

3. Cover and simmer for 15 to 20 minutes. Garnish with chopped coriander leaves and serve warm.

Servings: 6   Time: 30 min.

Nutritional analysis per serving:

Calories	162	(RDA% 8)
Protein	3 gm	(RDA% 7)
Carbohydrate	20 gm	
Fat	8 gm	

Zucchini Balls Curry

Louki Kofta Curry

2 cups grated zucchini
¾ cup soy flour
¼ cup chick-pea flour
2½ teaspoons salt (according to taste)
2 teaspoons chili powder (according to taste)
2 teaspoons fennel seeds
½ teaspoon turmeric powder
2 teaspoons ginger root
soy oil for deep-frying

Grind into a paste (for sauce)

2 large onions (optional)
3 large tomatoes
1½ teaspoons chili powder (according to taste)
2 teaspoons salt (according to taste)
2 tablespoons coriander powder
½ teaspoon turmeric powder

For seasoning (tarka)

3 tablespoons soy oil
2 bay leaves
½ teaspoon cumin seeds
1 teaspoon whole coriander
1 teaspoon whole coriander seed
pinch of asafetida

For decoration

1 tablespoon chopped green pepper
3 tablespoons fresh chopped coriander leaves
½ teaspoon garam masala

1. Squeeze the grated zucchini. Add all the ingredients for the kofta except oil. Mix well and form into 18 to 20 small balls.

2. Prepare the kofta as directed in Patta Gobhi Kofta Curry recipe by following steps 2, 3 and 4.

Servings: 8   Time: 60 min.

Nutritional analysis per serving:

Calories	166	(RDA% 8)
Protein	5 gm	(RDA% 12)
Carbohydrate	9 gm	
Fat	13 gm	

Mixed-Vegetable Curry
With Tofu
Navratan Curry

A majestic dish of North India, navratan curry combines fruits like pineapple and grapes with vegetables such as green beans and carrots in a sumptuous sauce. It makes a meal suited for royalty.

½ cup cut green beans
½ cup carrots, cut small
½ cup peas
¼ cup chopped green pepper
½ chopped apple
½ cup grapes
½ cup chopped pineapple
1 cup tofu, diced

For sauce

1 teaspoon chili powder (according to taste)
1½ teaspoons salt (according to taste)
1 teaspoon coriander powder
¼ teaspoon turmeric powder
2 teaspoons lemon juice
2 cups yogurt
1 tablespoon all-purpose flour or chick-pea flour
1½ cups water

For seasoning (tarka)

3 tablespoons soy oil
½ teaspoon cumin seeds
pinch of asafetida

For decoration

1 tablespoon chopped ginger
½ teaspoon garam masala
2 teaspoons chopped green pepper
3 tablespoons chopped green coriander leaves

1. Boil green beans, carrots and peas, and set aside. In a heavy pan heat soy oil. Add all the seasonings and fry for 30 seconds. Add tofu and fry for 4 minutes or until tofu becomes golden brown.

2. In a bowl mix all the ingredients for the sauce. Add this mixture to the pan. Cook on low heat, stirring constantly, until it comes to a boil. Boil for 2 to 3 minutes.

3. Add all the boiled vegetables, green pepper, and fruits, and cook for another 3 to 4 minutes. Mix in garam masala, garnish with coriander leaves, green pepper and chopped ginger, and serve warm.

Servings: 6   Time: 50 min.

Nutritional analysis per serving:

Calories	184	(RDA% 9)
Protein	7 gm	(RDA% 15)
Carbohydrate	17 gm	
Fat	11 gm	

Tofu Vegetable-Style
Tofu Sabji

Tofu sabji is a protein-packed dish with the sweetness of fresh cream, which creates a taste savored by all.

2 cups tofu, diced
½ cup fresh cream or light cream
5 tablespoons soy oil
½ teaspoon cumin seeds
3 tablespoons chopped coriander leaves
1 tablespoon chopped green pepper
pinch of asafetida

Grind into a paste (for sauce)

2 tomatoes (2 cups chopped)
2 tablespoons grated fresh coconut
1 stick cinnamon (1 inch)
3 cloves
4 teaspoons coriander powder
½ teaspoon red chili powder (according to taste)
1½ teaspoons cumin seeds
2 teaspoons chopped ginger
2 teaspoons salt (according to taste)
1½ tablespoons lemon juice

1. In a heavy pan heat soy oil. Add cumin seeds, asafetida, and tofu cubes and fry for 2 to 5 minutes. Add sauce paste and 1 cup water and cook for 3 to 5 minutes.
2. Add cream to the sauce and cook for 10 minutes. Serve warm garnished with coriander leaves and chopped green pepper.

Servings: 6   Time: 30 min.

Nutritional analysis per serving:

Calories	231	(RDA% 12)
Protein	6 gm	(RDA% 13)
Carbohydrate	5 gm	
Fat	22 gm	

Spinach
With Fried Tofu
Palak Paneer

Like matar paneer, palak paneer is another restaurant favorite. It is also a dish commonly prepared for holidays and parties.

½ pound fresh spinach
1 cup tofu, diced
4 tablespoons soy oil
½ teaspoon cumin seeds
½ teaspoon garam masala
pinch of asafetida
soy oil for deep-frying

Grind into a paste (for sauce)

1 cup chopped onions (optional)
1 cup chopped tomatoes
1 teaspoon chili powder (according to taste)
1½ teaspoons salt (according to taste)
2 teaspoons coriander powder
½ teaspoon turmeric powder
½ teaspoon cumin seeds
1 tablespoon thinly chopped ginger
2 green chilies
about ½ cup water

1. Wash the spinach and pick out only the leaves. Add ½ cup water and blend into a paste.
2. Deep-fry the tofu cubes in soy oil until they become light brown. Place cubes in a bowl of water to remove the oil.
3. In a heavy pan heat 4 tablespoons of oil and add cumin seeds and asafetida. Fry for a few seconds, then add sauce paste and cook for 8 to 10 minutes or until oil starts oozing out.
4. Add spinach paste and tofu cubes, and cook on low heat for 15 to 20 minutes. Add garam masala. Put in a serving plate and serve warm.

Servings: 4   Time: 30 min.

Nutritional analysis per serving:

Calories	229	(RDA% 11)
Protein	6 gm	(RDA% 14)
Carbohydrate	8 gm	
Fat	21 gm	

Mixed-Vegetable Korma
With Tofu

Mixed-vegetable korma with tofu is a simple and delicious dish to make when unexpected friends drop by for dinner. It is one preparation which combines most of the vegetables.

1 cup chopped tofu
1 cup potatoes, diced
½ cup radishes, peeled and cut in 1-inch pieces
½ cup squash cut in 1-inch pieces
½ cup carrots cut in 1-inch pieces
½ cup beans cut in small pieces

Grind into a paste (for sauce)

3 large tomatoes (2½ cups chopped tomatoes)
1 large chopped onion (optional)
1 teaspoon red pepper (according to taste)
2 teaspoons salt (according to taste)
2 green peppers, chopped
1 teaspoon cumin seeds
3 teaspoons coriander powder
½ teaspoon turmeric powder
1 tablespoon chopped ginger root

For seasoning (tarka)

½ cup soy oil
½ teaspoon cumin seeds
½ teaspoon mustard seeds
1 bay leaf
pinch of asafetida

For decoration

½ cup chopped coriander leaves

1. In a frying pan heat ¼ cup soy oil, add tofu cubes and fry for 5 to 6 minutes, or until they become light brown. Add all the vegetables and fry for 10 minutes, or until tender.

2. In a deep pan heat ¼ cup of soy oil. Add all the seasonings and fry for a few seconds. Then add the sauce paste, and cook for 7 to 8 minutes. Add 1 cup water and let it come to a boil. Add all the fried vegetables. Mix well; simmer for 8 to 10 minutes. Put in a serving plate; garnish with coriander leaves. Serve warm.

Servings: 6   Time: 40 min.

Nutritional analysis per serving:

Calories	259	(RDA% 13)
Protein	5 gm	(RDA% 11)
Carbohydrate	18 gm	
Fat	20 gm	

Cabbage
With Tofu
Patta Gobhi Sabji

Cabbage with tofu has a refreshing flavor and is nutritious as well.

4 cups cut cabbage
1 cup chopped tofu
½ teaspoon chili powder (according to taste)
2 teaspoons salt (according to taste)
2 teaspoons coriander powder
½ teaspoon turmeric powder
3 tablespoons soy oil
1 teaspoon mustard seeds
2 teaspoons chopped green pepper
3 tablespoons chopped coriander leaves
2 teaspoons chopped ginger root
pinch of asafetida

1. Heat the soy oil in a frying pan over medium heat. When it is hot, add asafetida and mustard seeds. Fry for a few seconds, then add chopped tofu and chopped ginger. Fry for 5 to 6 minutes. Add chopped cabbage and cook for 3 minutes on medium heat.

2. Add all the other ingredients except coriander leaves and green pepper. Stir well, cover and cook for 5 to 6 minutes, or until the cabbage is tender.

3. Garnish with coriander leaves and green pepper. Serve warm.

Servings: 6   Time: 20 min.

Nutritional analysis per serving:

Calories	96	(RDA% 5)
Protein	3 gm	(RDA% 7)
Carbohydrate	4 gm	
Fat	8 gm	

Spinach
With Tofu
Palak Sabji

4 cups chopped spinach
½ cup tofu
1 teaspoon chili powder (according to taste)
1 teaspoon salt (according to taste)
2 teaspoons coriander powder
½ teaspoon turmeric powder
½ teaspoon cumin seeds
1 teaspoon chopped ginger
1 large chopped tomato
3 tablespoons soy oil
pinch of asafetida

1. In a heavy pan heat soy oil. Add asafetida and cumin seeds and fry for a few seconds. Add ginger and tofu and cook for 3 to 4 minutes, until tofu becomes slightly brown. Then add tomato and cook for a few minutes.
2. Add spinach and all other ingredients. Stir well. Cover and cook on medium heat for 5 to 7 minutes, or until spinach is done.
3. Serve warm.

Servings: 6   Time: 20 min.

Nutritional analysis per serving:

Calories	79	(RDA% 4)
Protein	2 gm	(RDA% 5)
Carbohydrate	2 gm	
Fat	8 gm	

Fenugreek Leaves

With Soy Flour

Methi Sabji

4 cups fenugreek leaves, washed and chopped
¼ cup soy flour
¼ cup chick-pea flour
1 teaspoon chili powder (according to taste)
1½ teaspoons salt (according to taste)
1 teaspoon coriander powder
½ teaspoon turmeric powder
1 teaspoon chopped ginger
½ teaspoon cumin seeds
⅓ cup soy oil
pinch of asafetida

1. In a heavy pan heat soy oil. When heated, add asafetida and cumin seeds and fry for a few seconds. Add fenugreek leaves and all the other ingredients, stir well, cover, and cook on low heat for 4 to 5 minutes.
2. Stir a few times, scraping off all the chick-pea and soy flour that clings to the bottom of the pan.
3. Serve warm.

Servings: 6   Time: 20 min.

Nutritional analysis per serving:

Calories	145	(RDA% 7)
Protein	4 gm	(RDA% 8)
Carbohydrate	5 gm	
Fat	13 gm	

Radish Leaves

With Soy Flour

Mooli Patta Sabji

4 cups chopped radish leaves
½ cup soy flour or defatted soy flour
¼ cup chick-pea flour
1 teaspoon chili powder (according to taste)
1½ teaspoons salt (according to taste)
2 teaspoons coriander powder
½ teaspoon turmeric powder
½ teaspoon cumin seeds
½ cup soy oil
pinch of asafetida

1. In a heavy pan heat soy oil. Add asafetida and cumin seeds, and fry for a few seconds. Add radish leaves and salt, and cook for 3 minutes. Add all the other ingredients, stir well, cover, and cook on low heat for 4 to 5 minutes.

2. Stir a few times, scraping off all the chick-pea and soybean flour that clings to the bottom of the pan.

3. Serve warm.

Servings: 6   Time: 20 min.

Nutritional analysis per serving:

Calories	212	(RDA% 11)
Protein	5 gm	(RDA% 12)
Carbohydrate	17 gm	
Fat	19 gm	

Green Tomatoes
With Tofu
Katcha Tamatar with Tofu

3 cups green tomatoes, diced
1 cup chopped tofu
1 teaspoon salt (according to taste)
1 teaspoon chili powder (according to taste)
2 teaspoons coriander powder
½ teaspoon turmeric powder
4 tablespoons sugar (optional)
2 teaspoons chopped green pepper
2 tablespoons chopped coriander leaves

For seasoning (tarka)

3 tablespoons soy oil
½ teaspoon cumin seeds
pinch of asafetida

1. In a heavy pan heat the soy oil, add all the seasonings, and fry for a few minutes. Add chopped green tomatoes and cook for 8 to 10 minutes, until tomatoes are tender.
2. Add the other ingredients except chopped coriander leaves. Mix well. Cook for 2 minutes on low heat.
3. Garnish with coriander leaves. Serve warm.

Servings: 4   Time: 20 min.

Nutritional analysis per serving:

Calories	195	(RDA% 10)
Protein	5 gm	(RDA% 11)
Carbohydrate	19 gm	
Fat	12 gm	

Stuffed Potatoes

With Tofu

Bharwa Aloo

10 small potatoes

For filling

¾ cup tofu
½ cup grated coconut
1 teaspoon chili powder (according to taste)
2 teaspoons salt (according to taste)
3 teaspoons coriander powder
½ teaspoon turmeric powder
2 teaspoons fennel seeds
3 tablespoons chopped coriander leaves
2 teaspoons chopped green pepper
2 teaspoons chopped ginger

For seasoning (tarka)

½ teaspoon cumin seeds
½ teaspoon mustard seeds
½ cup soy oil
pinch of asafetida

For decoration

½ teaspoon garam masala
3 teaspoons mango powder (amchur)
3 tablespoons coriander leaves
2 teaspoons chopped green pepper
1 tomato, sliced
2 teaspoons chopped ginger
1 lemon, sliced

1. Peel the potatoes and prick holes in them with a sharp pointed knife or fork. Take out a round slice from top of each potato and set aside. Scoop out the insides with a sharp-pointed knife, set aside. Soak the potatoes until you are ready to cook.

2. In a bowl mix all the filling ingredients, adding the pieces that were removed from the insides of the potatoes.

3. Take the scooped-out potatoes from the water and drain them. Fill each potato with the filling. Close the openings of the potatoes with the round slices taken from the tops, and attach them with toothpicks.

4. In a heavy frying pan heat the soy oil, add all the seasoning ingredients, and fry for a few seconds. Arrange stuffed potatoes in the pan. Cook them on very low heat for 20 minutes. Turn them over and cook them about 20 minutes more or until done. Add the remaining filling and cook for 5 minutes, or until done. Add a little water, if it appears dry.

5. Add garam masala and mango powder; mix well. Transfer the potatoes to a serving plate. Decorate with tomato and lemon slices and other garnishes. Serve warm.

Servings: 8   Time: 50 min.

Nutritional analysis per serving:

Calories	311	(RDA% 16)
Protein	5 gm	(RDA% 11)
Carbohydrate	37 gm	
Fat	17 gm	

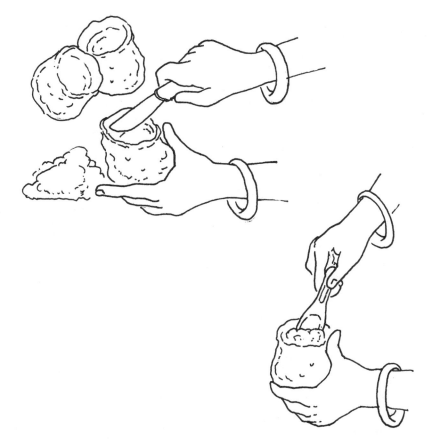

Stuffed Tomatoes
With Tofu
Bharwa Tamatar

6 medium size tomatoes

For filling

1 cup boiled mashed potatoes
½ cup coconut powder
½ cup tofu
2 teaspoons salt
½ teaspoon chili powder
2 tablespoons cashew nuts
2 tablespoons raisins
¼ teaspoon turmeric powder

Grind into a paste (for the sauce)

2 large tomatoes
1 small onion (optional)
3 green chilies (optional)
1 tablespoon chopped ginger
1 teaspoon chili powder (according to taste)
2½ teaspoons salt (according to taste)
½ teaspoon turmeric
3 tablespoons coriander powder

For seasoning (tarka)

2 large cardamoms
2 sticks of cinnamon
1 bay leaf
2 cloves
½ teaspoon mustard seeds
½ teaspoon cumin seeds
3 tablespoons soy oil
pinch of asafetida

For decoration

3 tablespoons finely chopped coriander leaves
¾ teaspoon garam masala

1. Wash the tomatoes and remove a slice from the top of each tomato. Set these slices aside. Scoop out the inside pulp of the tomatoes with a sharp knife.
2. Mix all the filling ingredients. Stuff the tomatoes with the filling, cover with slices cut earlier, and attach with a toothpick.

3. Heat soy oil in a wide frying pan. Then put all the seasonings into it and fry for a few seconds. Add sauce paste and the tomato pulp that was removed from scooped tomatoes. Cook for 7 to 8 minutes.
4. Add 2 to 3 cups water and cook for 5 minutes on medium heat. Arrange the tomatoes in the prepared sauce. Sprinkle with leftover filling and cook over medium heat for 10 minutes.
5. Add garam masala. Decorate with coriander leaves and other garnishes, and serve warm.

Servings: 6   Time: 50 min.

Nutritional analysis per serving:

Calories	220	(RDA% 11)
Protein	5 gm	(RDA% 11)
Carbohydrate	26 gm	
Fat	11 gm	

Stuffed Eggplants

With Tofu

Bharwa Baingan

10 small eggplants

For filling

¾ cup tofu
1 teaspoon chili powder (according to taste)
3 teaspoons salt (according to taste)
2 tablespoons coriander seeds
½ teaspoon turmeric powder
¼ cup poppy seeds
¼ cup white sesame seeds
3 tablespoons chopped coriander leaves
2 teaspoons chopped green pepper
2 teaspoons chopped ginger
3 teaspoons mango powder (amchur)

For seasoning (tarka)

½ teaspoon cumin seeds
½ teaspoon mustard seeds
½ cup soy oil
pinch of asafetida

For decoration

3 tablespoons coriander leaves
2 teaspoons chopped green pepper
1 tomato, sliced
2 teaspoons chopped ginger
1 lemon, sliced

1. Wash the eggplants. Make a slit through the middle without breaking them, and put in water while you prepare the filling.
2. Put a frying pan on low heat without oil. Roast dry coriander seeds, poppy seeds and sesame seeds one after another. Grind all roasted seeds in a blender and mix with other filling ingredients.
3. Take the eggplants out of the water and drain them. Fill each baingan with the filling.
4. In a heavy frying pan heat the soy oil, add all the seasonings and fry for a few seconds. Arrange stuffed baingan in the frying pan and cook on very low heat for 20 minutes. Turn them over and cook until they are done. Add the remaining filling and cook for 5 minutes or until done. Add a little water if dry.

5. Arrange bharwa baingan on a serving plate. Decorate with tomato, lemon slices and the garnishes. Serve warm.

Servings: 6   Time: 50 min.

Nutritional analysis per serving:

Calories	258	(RDA% 13)
Protein	4 gm	(RDA% 10)
Carbohydrate	12 gm	
Fat	22 gm	

Stuffed Zucchini
With Tofu
Bharwa Louki

8 1½ inch long zucchini pieces, peeled
1 teaspoon salt

For filling

1 cup mashed tofu
1½ cups boiled mashed potatoes
1 cup boiled mixed vegetables (peas, corn, beans and carrots)
2 teaspoons salt (according to taste)
½ teaspoon chili powder (according to taste)
¼ teaspoon turmeric powder
1½ teaspoons mango powder (amchur)

Grind into a paste (for the sauce)

2 large tomatoes
1 tablespoon chopped ginger
2 green peppers, chopped
1 teaspoon chili powder
1½ teaspoons salt
3 teaspoons coriander powder
½ teaspoon turmeric powder
2 tablespoons lemon juice

For seasoning (tarka)

¼ cup soy oil
2 cinnamon sticks
2 bay leaves
4 cloves
½ teaspoon mustard seeds
½ teaspoon cumin seeds
pinch of asafetida

For decoration

½ teaspoon garam masala
½ cup chopped coriander leaves

1. Wash the zucchini pieces and scoop out the seeds with a sharp knife. In a big pot add water, louki pieces and 1 teaspoon salt, and boil until louki become slightly soft. Take louki out of the water and allow to cool.
2. Mix all the ingredients for the filling and stuff the zucchini pieces with the mixture.

3. Heat the soy oil in a wide frying pan, then add all the seasonings and fry for a few seconds. Add the sauce and cook at medium heat for 7 to 8 minutes until oil starts oozing out.

4. Add 2 cups water and leftover filling and cook for 5 minutes on medium heat. Arrange the stuffed louki in the prepared sauce and cook for 5 minutes.

5. Arrange in a serving dish. Decorate with coriander leaves and garam masala and serve warm.

Servings: 6   Time: 50 min.

Nutritional analysis per serving:

Calories	234	(RDA% 12)
Protein	7 gm	(RDA% 15)
Carbohydrate	30 gm	
Fat	11 gm	

Stuffed Onions

With Soy Okra

Bharwa Pyaz

10 small onions

For filling

½ cup soy okra
¼ cup grated coconut
½ teaspoon chili powder (according to taste)
1½ teaspoons salt (according to taste)
3 teaspoons coriander powder
½ teaspoon turmeric powder
2 teaspoons chopped ginger

Grind into a paste (for the sauce)

2 large tomatoes
1 tablespoon chopped ginger
2 green peppers
1 teaspoon chili powder (according to taste)
1½ teaspoons salt
1 teaspoon garam masala
½ teaspoon turmeric powder

For seasoning (tarka)

¼ cup soy oil
2 bay leaves
½ teaspoon mustard seeds
3 tablespoons chopped coriander leaves
pinch of asafetida

1. Clean the onions and make two perpendicular slits in each without slicing them. In a bowl mix all the filling ingredients and stuff each onion.

2. Heat the soy oil in a wide frying pan, add all the seasonings, and fry for a few seconds. Then add sauce paste and cook for 7 to 8 minutes, until oil starts oozing out.

3. Add 1 cup water and cook for 5 minutes on medium heat. Arrange the stuffed onions in the prepared sauce. Sprinkle with leftover filling and cook on medium heat for 20 minutes or until onions are done. Garnish with coriander leaves; serve warm.

Servings: 6   Time: 50 min.

Nutritional analysis per serving:

Calories	168	(RDA% 8)
Protein	3 gm	(RDA% 6)
Carbohydrate	16 gm	
Fat	11 gm	

Stuffed Bananas
With Tofu
Bharwa Kela

10 1½ inch pieces of ripe bananas

For filling

½ cup mashed tofu
½ cup coconut powder
1 teaspoon chili powder (according to taste)
2 teaspoons salt (according to taste)
3 teaspoons coriander powder
2 teaspoons mango powder (amchur)
½ teaspoon turmeric powder
3 teaspoons chopped green pepper
½ cup chopped coriander leaves

For seasoning (tarka)

½ cup soy oil
½ teaspoon cumin seeds
½ teaspoon mustard seeds
pinch of asafetida

For garnish

1 tablespoon chopped coriander leaves

1. Wash the bananas and make a longitudinal slit in each piece, with the skin still on them.
2. Mix all the ingredients for the filling and stuff the banana pieces.
3. In a wide frying pan heat the soy oil, add all the seasonings, and fry briefly. Arrange all the stuffed bananas in the pan.
4. Cover and cook for 4 minutes on low heat, then turn the bananas over very carefully. Sprinkle with leftover filling. Cover and cook again for 3 to 4 minutes or until done.
5. Arrange on a serving plate, garnish with coriander leaves, and serve warm with bread. The banana skin can also be eaten.

Servings: 6   Time: 25 min.

Nutritional analysis per serving:

Calories	265	(RDA% 13)
Protein	2 gm	(RDA% 5)
Carbohydrate	18 gm	
Fat	21 gm	

Stuffed Bell Peppers
With Tofu
Bharwa Mirch

6 medium size bell peppers (sweet peppers)

For filling

1 cup mashed tofu
2 cups boiled and diced potatoes
1 cup boiled peas
2 teaspoons salt (according to taste)
1 teaspoon chili powder (according to taste)
2 teaspoons coriander powder
½ teaspoon turmeric powder
3 teaspoons mango powder (amchur)
½ teaspoon garam masale
4 tablespoons chopped coriander leaves
3 teaspoons chopped ginger
2 tablespoons chopped cashew nuts
2 tablespoons raisins
2 tablespoons walnuts (optional)

For seasoning (tarka)

½ teaspoon cumin seeds
½ teaspoon mustard seeds
¼ cup soy oil
pinch of asafetida

For decoration

4 tablespoons chopped
coriander leaves
1 tomato sliced
1 lemon sliced
2 carrots cut in 2-inch lengths

1. Wash the bell peppers and cut each into equal pieces. Remove all the seeds. Boil the bell peppers for about 5 minutes, then drain.

2. In a heavy frying pan heat soy oil, add asafetida and mustard seeds, fry for a few seconds. Then add chopped tofu and fry until light brown. Add cashews, walnuts, and raisins and fry for a few more seconds. Add all other ingredients, mix well and cook for another 2 to 3 minutes.

3. Stuff the bell peppers with the potato and tofu filling. Arrange them in a greased casserole dish. Bake at 350 F for 10 to 15 minutes, or until tender.

4. Garnish with tomato and lemon slices, carrots and chopped coriander leaves. Serve warm with any type of bread.

Servings: 6   Time: 50 min.

Nutritional analysis per serving:

Calories	276	(RDA% 14)
Protein	7 gm	(RDA% 17)
Carbohydrate	34 gm	
Fat	13 gm	

Stuffed Cucumbers
With Tofu
Bharwa Kakri

10 small tender pickle cucumbers

For filling

¾ cup mashed tofu
1 teaspoon chili powder (according to taste)
2 teaspoons salt (according to taste)
3 teaspoons coriander powder
⅓ teaspoon turmeric powder
½ teaspoon cumin seeds
3 teaspoons mango powder (amchur)
2 teaspoons chopped ginger
4 tablespoons chopped coriander leaves
¼ cup soy oil
pinch of asafetida

1. Chop off a slice from one end of each cucumber and scoop out the seeds carefully.
2. Mix all the ingredients for the filling except oil, cumin seeds, asafetida, and 2 tablespoons of coriander leaves. Fill each cucumber with this mixture.
3. In a heavy wide frying pan heat the oil. When oil is hot add cumin seeds and asafetida, and fry for a few seconds. Add all the stuffed cucumbers, cover, and cook on low heat. Cook for 10 to 15 minutes. Turn the cucumbers over. Add the remaining filling and cook until they are done.
4. Take out and arrange on a serving dish and garnish with remaining coriander leaves. Serve warm.

Servings: 6   Time: 50 min.

Nutritional analysis per serving:

Calories	118	(RDA% 6)
Protein	3 gm	(RDA% 6)
Carbohydrate	5 gm	
Fat	10 gm	

Hot Small Chilies

Stuffed with Soy Flour

Hot Bharwa Mirch

15 to 20 hot green chilies

For filling

½ cup soy flour
3 teaspoons coriander powder
½ teaspoon turmeric powder
2 tablespoons salt (according to taste)
2 teaspoons fennel seeds
3 teaspoons mango powder (amchur)
½ teaspoon cumin seeds
pinch of asafetida
4 tablespoons chopped coriander leaves
½ cup soy oil

1. Wash green chilies and make a slit in one side. In a bowl mix all the other ingredients except oil, cumin seeds, asafetida and coriander leaves. Stuff all the chilies.

2. Heat the soy oil in a wide heavy frying pan. When oil is hot, add cumin seeds and asafetida. Fry them for a few seconds. Arrange the stuffed chilies in the pan. Lower the heat, cover, and cook for 5 minutes. Turn the chilies over, add all the remaining filling, and cook for another 5 minutes, or until done.

3. Arrange them in a serving dish. Garnish with coriander leaves, and serve warm.

Servings: 6   Time: 50 min.

Nutritional analysis per serving:

Calories	225	(RDA% 11)
Protein	4 gm	(RDA% 8)
Carbohydrate	9 gm	
Fat	19 gm	

Stuffed Tinda

With Tofu

Though difficult to find in America, tinda are a common vegetable in India. They are round about the size of a tomato and have the firm texture of cucumbers.

8 to 10 medium size tinda

For filling

½ cup tofu
¼ cup coconut powder
1 teaspoon salt (according to taste)
1 teaspoon chili powder (according to taste)
2 teaspoons cashew nuts
2 teaspoons raisins
¼ teaspoon turmeric powder

Grind into a paste (for the sauce)

1 large size tomato or 1 cup chopped tomatoes
1 small onion (optional)
3 green chilies (according to taste)
1 tablespoon chopped ginger
½ teaspoon chili powder (according to taste)
2 teaspoons salt (according to taste)
2 teaspoons coriander powder

For seasoning (tarka)

4 tablespoons soy oil
2 big cardamoms
1 bay leaf
pinch of asafetida
½ teaspoon mustard seeds
½ teaspoon cumin seeds

For decoration

½ cup finely chopped coriander leaves
½ teaspoon garam masala

1. Wash and peel the tinda. Remove a slice from the top of each tinda; set aside. Scoop out the inside seeds with a sharp knife.
2. Mix all the filling ingredients, stuff each tinda with the filling and cover with the slice that was removed from the top. Attach with toothpicks.
3. Heat soy oil in a wide frying pan. Then put all the seasonings into it and fry for a few seconds. Add sauce paste and cook for 7 to 8 minutes.

4. Add 1 cup water and cook for 5 minutes on medium heat. Arrange the tinda in the prepared sauce. Sprinkle with leftover filling and cook over medium heat for 15 to 20 minutes.

5. Take them out in a serving dish. Garnish with coriander leaves, sprinkle garam masala and serve warm.

Servings: 6   Time: 50 min.

Nutritional analysis per serving:

Calories	142	(RDA% 7)
Protein	4 gm	(RDA% 8)
Carbohydrate	8 gm	
Fat	11 gm	

Sweet-and-Sour Bitter Melons
Stuffed with Soy Flour
Khatta Mitha Karela

Ingredients same as in previous recipe
5 teaspoons sugar or brown sugar

1. Prepare all the ingredients as in the previous recipe for stuffed karela.

2. In a heavy frying pan heat the oil and add cumin seeds and asafetida. Then add the bharwa karela. Cover them and cook on low heat for 10 minutes. Add 5 teaspoons sugar or brown sugar. Cook for another 5 minutes. Serve cold or hot.

Note: In place of soy flour ½ cup tofu can be used for the filling.

Servings: 6   Time: 50 min.

Nutritional analysis per serving:

Calories	200	(RDA% 10)
Protein	4 gm	(RDA% 9)
Carbohydrate	6 gm	
Fat	18 gm	

Stuffed Bitter Melon
With Tofu
Bharwa Karela

4 medium sized karela (bitter melon), or 10 to 14 one inch pieces

For filling

¾ cup tofu
1 teaspoon chili powder (according to taste)
3 teaspoons coriander powder
2 teaspoons salt (according to taste)
½ teaspoon turmeric powder
2 teaspoons mango powder (amchur)
2 teaspoons fennel seeds
½ teaspoon cumin seeds
2 teaspoons chopped ginger
½ cup soy oil
pinch of asafetida
3 teaspoons salt for rubbing

1. Scrape the karela and set the skin aside (if it is good). Make a slit on one side of each karela; if seeds are not good take them out. Take the 3 teaspoons of salt and rub it into the inside and outside of the karela. Set aside for 1 to 2 hours to remove the bitter taste.
2. Mix all the other ingredients except the oil, cumin seeds and asafetida. Wash and squeeze the karela and stuff each of them with the filling; if desired you can wrap each bitter melon with a string.
3. Heat the soy oil in a wide frying pan, and add cumin seeds and asafetida. Then add the stuffed karela and cook them on low heat for 10 minutes. Turn them over, sprinkle with leftover filling, and cook until they are done.
4. Serve the bharwa karela cold or hot.

Note: In place of tofu, ½ cup soy flour can be used for the filing.

Servings: 6   Time: 50 min.

Nutritional analysis per serving:

Calories	200	(RDA% 10)
Protein	4 gm	(RDA% 9)
Carbohydrate	6 gm	
Fat	18 gm	

Stuffed Okra
With Soy Flour
Bharwa Bhindi

1 pound tender okra
¼ cup soy flour
1½ teaspoons salt (according to taste)
1 teaspoon chili (according to taste)
2 teaspoons coriander powder
⅓ teaspoon turmeric powder
2 teaspoons mango powder (amchur)
½ teaspoon cumin seeds
pinch of asafetida
⅓ cup soy oil
1 teaspoon chopped ginger
3 tablespoons chopped coriander leaves

1. Wash the okras and dry them with a cloth or paper towel. Make a slit on one side of each okra.
2. Mix all the other ingredients except oil, cumin seeds, coriander leaves and asafetida. Stuff the okra with the filling.
3. Heat the soy oil in a wide frying pan. Add asafetida and cumin seeds and fry briefly. Then add okra, cover, and cook for 5 minutes on low heat. Turn them over, and sprinkle with leftover filling and cook until done.
4. Garnish with coriander leaves. Serve warm with bread.

Servings: 6   Time: 50 min.

Nutritional analysis per serving:

Calories	214	(RDA% 11)
Protein	5 gm	(RDA% 10)
Carbohydrate	10 gm	
Fat	18 gm	

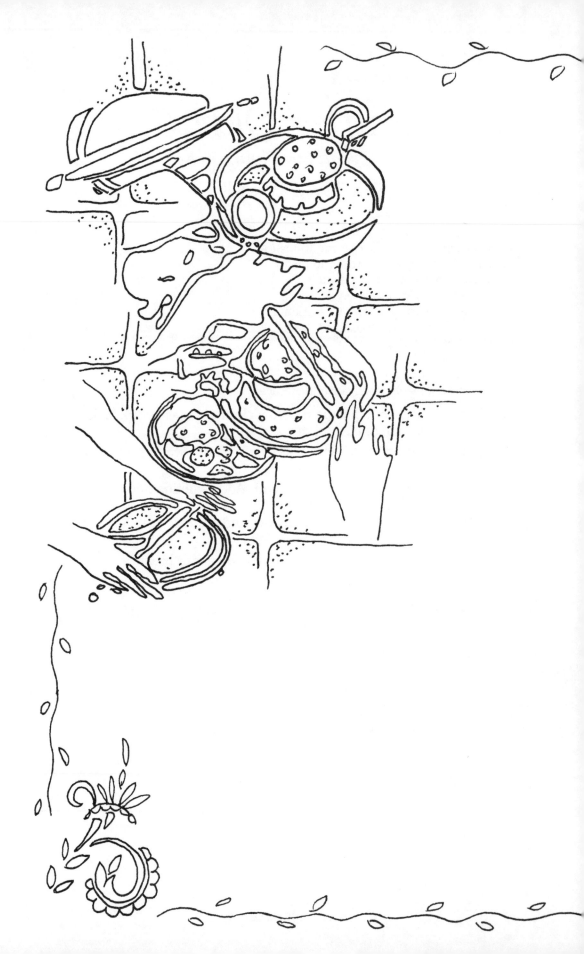

Soy Breads

IN INDIA bread is made at home not just on special occasions, but every day, even twice a day. It is no wonder that the variety of bread recipes is endless. Chappati is the most humble of Indian breads; it is flat, round and baked on a cast-iron skillet or frying pan. Customarily, chappati is made from whole-wheat flour, but we have added 25 percent soy flour which doubles the protein content, yet still maintains the traditional taste and soft texture.

Poori is the most delightful of Indian breads. It is deep-fried and it fascinates all by ballooning into a size of a grapefruit. It is the bread of choice for parties, to be served with vegetable dishes.

Like chappatis, parathas are baked in a skillet; however, layers of oil are added to the dough while rolling, which adds a sweet fried taste. Often parathas are stuffed with vegetables, and we have added tofu for a nutritious delight. Parathas, when eaten with raita or chutney, can make a whole meal.

Often milk is added to the dough. In some of these recipes we have added soy okra and tofu, which soften the dough and make a more nutritious bread.

A Combine whole-wheat, soy flour and salt in a bowl.

B Knead to make smooth dough.

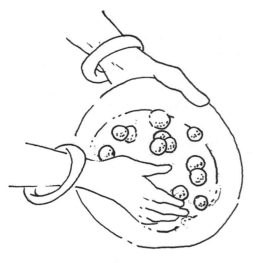

C Divide dough into 10-12 equal balls.

D Roll on lightly floured surface to a circle of 5-7 inch diameter.

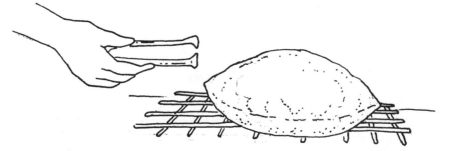

E After cooking on a skillet for 1 minute place on a screen or gas burner until the chapatti puffs.

Chapatti

Chappati

The mainstay of the North Indian meal is chappati. In our home in Boston, it is baked fresh every evening for dinner, and in India it is baked twice a day. Though it may appear difficult, it is really very easy to make. Chappati is broken into bite size pieces and eaten with vegetables and lentils, making a delicious combination. It is the cornerstone of the Indian meal.

1½ cups whole-wheat flour
½ cup soy flour
½ teaspoon salt
about ¾ cup water
butter for top

1. Combine whole-wheat flour, soy flour, and salt in a bowl and mix well. Add enough water to make a soft dough. Knead for a few minutes until dough becomes smooth. Then cover the bowl and set aside at room temperature for 10 to 15 minutes.

2. Knead again for 2 to 3 minutes; if it sticks add ½ teaspoon oil. Then divide the dough into 10 to 12 equal portions and shape into round balls. Sprinkle with flour and roll out on a lightly floured surface to 5 to 7 inches in diameter.

3. Heat a heavy skillet or flat frying pan and place one chappati on it. Cook for 1 minute or less on each side, until it is firm to the touch. Then place the chappati on a screen or rack and hold over the flame of a gas burner, or over an electric burner on high heat, for 3 to 5 seconds, or until the bread puffs. Use tongs with rounded ends to turn the chappati. Make sure it does not burn. Serve warm with butter on top. Repeat to make all the chappatis.

Servings: 4   Time: 25 min.

Nutritional analysis per serving:

Calories	174	(RDA% 9)
Protein	6 gm	(RDA% 14)
Carbohydrate	25 gm	
Fat	6 gm	

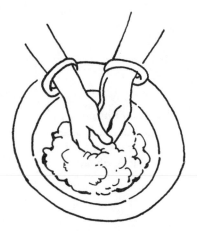

A Combine whole-wheat flour, soy flour, and salt in a bowl.

B Knead to make a stiff dough.

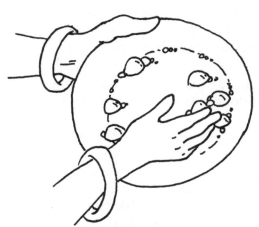

C Divide dough into 18-20 balls.

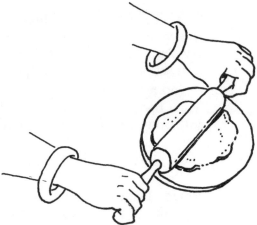

D Roll on oiled surface to a circle of 4-inch diameter.

E Deep fry until pori puffs or turns golden brown.

Poori

Deep-Fried Whole-Wheat Soy Bread

Soy Poori

Pooris are "pillow breads" or "balloon breads," because when they are fried they blow up like balloons, which awes our American friends. Warm pooris are a treat for special occasions with guests.

1½ cups whole-wheat flour
½ cup soy flour
About ½ cup water
Soy oil for deep-frying

1. Combine whole-wheat flour, soy flour and salt in a bowl. Add enough water to make a very stiff dough. Knead for a few minutes, then cover the bowl and set aside at room temperature for 10 to 15 minutes.

2. Knead again for 2 to 3 minutes; if it sticks add ½ teaspoon oil. Then divide the dough into 18 to 20 balls. Roll them to 4 inches in diameter. If dough is sticky add a little oil or flour and roll.

3. Heat the soy oil in a deep frying pan. When hot, drop in one poori at a time. Press it lightly with the back of a slotted spoon so it puffs completely. Fry poori on both sides for only a few seconds or until golden brown. Remove with a slotted spoon and drain on a paper towel. Serve hot. The pooris can be kept warm by wrapping them in aluminum foil.

Servings: 4   Time: 25 min.

Nutritional analysis per serving:

Calories	317	(RDA% 16)
Protein	9 gm	(RDA% 21)
Carbohydrate	37 gm	
Fat	15 gm	

Fried Whole-Wheat Soy Bread

Soy Paratha

For a Sunday afternoon picnic, parathas are our favorite choice of bread. Since they are skillet-fried, they can be preserved well and can be kept two to three days without refrigeration. Like chappati, they are broken into bite size pieces and eaten with vegetables.

1½ cups whole-wheat flour
½ teaspoon salt
½ cup soy flour
about ¾ cup water
soy oil or butter for frying

1. Combine whole-wheat flour, soy flour, and salt in a bowl and mix well. Add enough water to make a soft dough. Knead for a few minutes until dough becomes smooth.

2. Knead the dough for 2 minutes; if it sticks, add ½ teaspoon oil. Divide dough into 12 equal portions and shape into balls. Sprinkle with a little flour and roll out each ball on a lightly floured surface to 4 inches in diameter. Brush the butter or oil on top of the bread and fold it in half. Again brush with oil or butter and fold the bread to make a four-layered quarter circle. Roll it in triangular shape to 5 to 6 inches in diameter.

3. Heat a heavy skillet or flat frying pan and place one of the parathas on it. Cook for ½ minute. With a wide spatula turn paratha over and grease the top with one teaspoon oil or butter. Turn it over again and grease with one teaspoon oil or butter. Press with the spatula making sure all sides are fried properly. Fry for a few more minutes until both sides become golden.

4. Serve warm with curry or lentil soup.

Servings: 4   Time: 25 min.

Nutritional analysis per serving:

Calories	317	(RDA% 16)
Protein	9 gm	(RDA% 21)
Carbohydrate	37 gm	
Fat	15 gm	

Spicy Soy Bread
Micci Bread

Micci bread is spicy bread enjoyed with pickles and yogurt.

1 cup whole-wheat flour
½ cup soy flour
¼ cup chick-pea flour
1 teaspoon salt (according to taste)
1 teaspoon chili powder (according to taste)
1 teaspoon ajwain
4 teaspoons oil
about ¾ cup water
butter for top

1. Combine all the ingredients in a bowl except butter and mix well. Add enough water to make a dough. Cover the bowl and set aside at room temperature for 10 minutes.
2. Knead for 2 to 3 minutes; if it sticks add ½ teaspoon oil, then divide into 8 to 10 equal portions and shape into round balls.
3. Sprinkle with a little flour and roll out each ball on a lightly floured surface to 5 inches in diameter. Then follow the procedure for making whole-wheat chappati.

Servings: 4   Time: 30 min.

Nutritional analysis per serving:

Calories	235	(RDA% 12)
Protein	9 gm	(RDA% 21)
Carbohydrate	30 gm	
Fat	9 gm	

Crisp Puffed Soy Bread
Soy Naan

Naan is the favorite bread of Punjab, a prosperous state in North India. The village women bake the bread in a common clay oven and bring the warm bread back to their homes for dinner.

For dough

2½ cups all-purpose flour
½ cup soy flour
2 teaspoons baking powder
½ cup soy yogurt or plain yogurt
3 teaspoons butter
2 teaspoons sugar
1 teaspoon salt
½ cup soy milk or plain milk (optional)
butter for topping

1. Combine all the ingredients for the dough, except milk, in a bowl and mix well. Add milk and enough water to make a soft dough. Knead for a few minutes until dough becomes smooth. Then cover the bowl and keep it in a warm place for 3 to 4 hours.

2. Divide the dough into 10 to 12 equal portions and shape into round balls. Sprinkle with a little flour and roll out each ball on a lightly floured surface to about 4 to 5 inches in diameter.

3. Preheat the oven to broil temperature setting. Put two ungreased baking trays into the oven to preheat. Place 2 to 3 naans on the hot trays. Bake for few minutes or until bread is golden and puffed. Put butter on top and serve warm.

Servings: 4   Time: 30 min.

Nutritional analysis per serving:

Calories	388	(RDA% 19)
Protein	14 gm	(RDA% 31)
Carbohydrate	66 gm	
Fat	8 gm	

Fried All-Purpose Flour Soy Bread
Bhatura

Bhatura is deep-fried pita bread best enjoyed with chick-peas. In India it's fun to have cholla (chick-peas) and bhatura on a family outing.

2 cups all-purpose flour
½ cup soy flour
½ cup soy yogurt (if unavailable, may use ½ cup plain yogurt)
½ cup plain yogurt
1 teaspoon salt
1 teaspoon butter
½ teaspoon soda bicarbonate
5 teaspoons warm water
soy oil for deep-frying

1. Mix all the ingredients together except water and oil for frying. Add enough water to make a dough. Knead for 5 to 8 minutes. Cover the dough and set aside in a warm place for 2 to 3 hours. Divide into 12 to 14 equal portions, and shape into round balls.
2. Roll out each ball to 3 to 4 inches in diameter; if dough is sticky, add a little oil or flour and roll.
3. Heat the soy oil in a deep frying pan. When hot, fry one bhatura at a time. Press them lightly with the back of a slotted spoon so they puff completely. Fry bhaturas on both sides for only a few seconds, or until golden brown. Remove with a slotted spoon and drain on a paper towel. Serve hot.

Servings: 4   Time: 30 min.

Nutritional analysis per serving:

Calories	390	(RDA% 19)
Protein	12 gm	(RDA% 27)
Carbohydrate	49 gm	
Fat	16 gm	

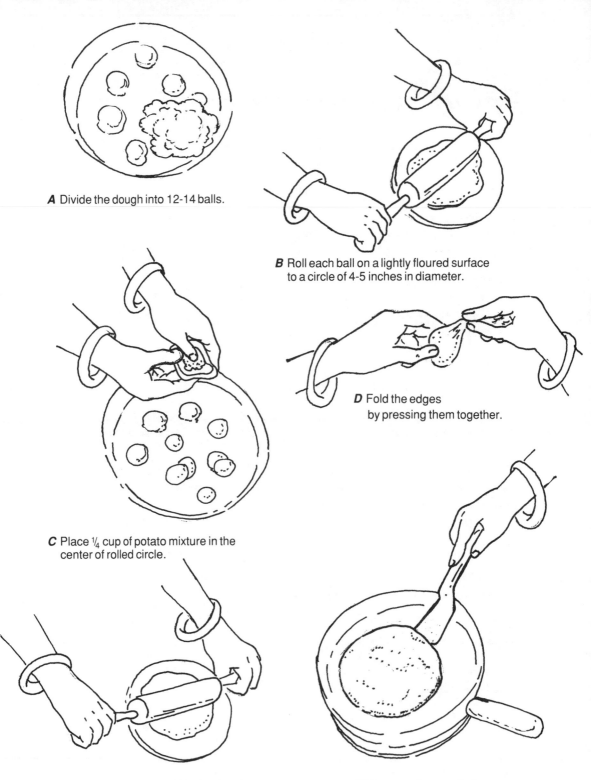

A Divide the dough into 12-14 balls.

B Roll each ball on a lightly floured surface to a circle of 4-5 inches in diameter.

C Place ¼ cup of potato mixture in the center of rolled circle.

D Fold the edges by pressing them together.

E Roll again with filling inside the dough.

F Heat paratha on a frying pan.

Aloo Paratha

Bread
Stuffed with Potatoes and Tofu
Aloo Paratha

My son, who enjoys french fries, is an aloo paratha lover. Paratha is a pleasant change from chappati, and the varieties of stuffings such as potatoes, peas, cabbage, or spinach allow you to modify the paratha to your taste. Paratha with chutney or cucumber raita makes a hearty meal.

For dough

2 cups whole-wheat flour
1 teaspoon salt
about 1 cup water
soy oil for frying

For filling

1 cup mashed tofu
2½ cups boiled mashed potatoes
3 teaspoons salt (according to taste)
2 teaspoons chili powder (according to taste)
1 teaspoon cumin seeds
2 teaspoons fennel seeds
2 tablespoons chopped green pepper
4 tablespoons chopped green coriander leaves
½ teaspoon garam masala
pinch of asafetida

1. Combine all the ingredients for the dough in a bowl, except soy oil, and mix well. Add enough water to make a dough. Cover the bowl and set aside at room temperature for 20 minutes. In another bowl mix all the ingredients for the filling.

2. Knead the dough for 2 minutes; if it sticks, add ½ teaspoon oil. Divide the dough into 12 to 14 equal portions and shape into balls. Sprinkle a little flour and roll out each ball on a lightly floured surface to 4 inches in diameter. Place ¼ cup of potato mixture in the center of the circle and fold the edges over by pressing them together to enclose the filling. Press by hand and roll again to make a 5 to 6 inch circle. Roll carefully, so that the filling remains inside.

3. Heat a heavy skillet or frying pan. Place one potato-filled paratha in the pan and cook for ½ minute. With a wide spatula turn paratha over and grease the top with one teaspoon oil. Turn it over again and grease with one teaspoon oil; let it cook for one minute. Fry for a few more minutes until both sides become golden.

4. Fry the other parathas in the same manner. Each paratha will take about 2 to 3 minutes to cook. Serve warm with chutney and raita.

Servings: 8   Time: 50 min.

Nutritional analysis per serving:

Calories	305	(RDA% 15)
Protein	9 gm	(RDA% 20)
Carbohydrate	34 gm	
Fat	15 gm	

Bread
Stuffed with Cauliflower and Tofu
Gobhi Paratha

For dough

2 cups whole-wheat flour
¼ teaspoon salt
about 1 cup water
soy oil for frying

For filling

2 cups grated cauliflower
1 cup tofu
2 teaspoons salt
1 teaspoon chili powder
2 teaspoons fennel seeds
4 teaspoons green pepper, chopped
1 small onion cut into small pieces
4 teaspoons chopped green coriander leaves

1. Combine all the ingredients for the dough, except oil, in a bowl and mix well. Add enough water to make a dough. Cover the bowl and set aside at room temperature for 20 minutes.
2. In another bowl mix all the ingredients for the filling.
3. Make cauliflower paratha in the same manner as aloo paratha.

Servings: 4   Time: 50 min.

Nutritional analysis per serving:

Calories	363	(RDA% 18)
Protein	10 gm	(RDA% 22)
Carbohydrate	45 gm	
Fat	16 gm	

Bread

Stuffed with Radishes and Tofu
Mooli Paratha

For dough

> 2 cups whole-wheat flour
> ½ teaspoon salt
> about 1 cup water
> soy oil for frying

For filling

> 2 cups grated radishes
> 1 cup mashed tofu
> 1½ teaspoons salt
> 1 teaspoon chili powder
> 1 teaspoon cumin seeds
> 2 teaspoons fennel seeds
> 2 tablespoons chopped green coriander leaves
> 1 tablespoon chopped green pepper
> 1 teaspoon chopped ginger

1. Combine all the ingredients for the dough in a bowl, except soy oil. Add enough water to make a dough. Knead for a few minutes. Cover the bowl and set aside at room temperature for 20 minutes.

2. Knead again for 2 to 3 minutes; if it sticks, add ½ teaspoon oil. Then divide the dough into 10 to 12 equal portions and shape into round balls.

3. Squeeze the radishes hard to extract the water, and mix well with all the other ingredients.

4. Make the mooli paratha in the same manner as aloo paratha. Serve warm with raita and chutney.

Servings: 4   Time: 50 min.

Nutritional analysis per serving:

Calories	381	(RDA% 19)
Protein	10 gm	(RDA% 23)
Carbohydrate	49 gm	
Fat	17 gm	

Bread
Stuffed with Peas and Tofu
Matar Paratha

For dough

> 2 cups whole-wheat flour
> 1 teaspoon salt
> about 1 cup water
> soy oil for frying

For filling

> 1 cup mashed tofu
> 4 cups green peas
> 3 teaspoons salt (according to taste)
> 1½ teaspoons chili powder (according to taste)
> 1 teaspoon cumin seeds
> 3 teaspoons fennel seeds
> 1 teaspoon garam masala
> 2 tablespoons chopped green pepper
> 1 tablespoon chopped ginger
> 4 tablespoons chopped green coriander leaves
> 4 tablespoons soy oil
> pinch of asafetida

1. Wash the peas well and blend into a coarse paste.
2. In a heavy frying pan heat 4 tablespoons oil. Add cumin seeds and asafetida; fry for a few seconds. Add the crushed peas and mashed tofu to the pan. Fry for 30 minutes on medium heat or until paste becomes thick and cooked. Add all other ingredients and mix well. Make 10 to 12 small balls.
3. Combine whole-wheat flour and salt in a bowl and mix well. Add enough water to make a soft dough. Knead for a few minutes until dough becomes smooth. Then cover the bowl and set aside at room temperature for 10 to 15 minutes.
4. Knead again for 2 to 3 minutes; if it sticks, add ½ teaspoon oil. Then divide the dough into 10 to 12 equal portions and shape into round balls. Sprinkle with a little flour and roll out on a lightly floured surface to 4 inches in diameter. Place ball of filling in the center of the circle and fold the edges over by pressing them together to enclose the filling. Press by hand and roll again to make a 5- to 6-inch round paratha. Roll carefully, so that the filling remains inside.

5. Fry all the paratha in the same manner as aloo paratha. Serve warm with chutney and yogurt.

Servings: 8   Time: 70 min.

Nutritional analysis per serving:

Calories	215	(RDA% 11)
Protein	4 gm	(RDA% 9)
Carbohydrate	33 gm	
Fat	7 gm	

Spinach Bread
With Soy Okra
Palak Paratha

2 cups whole-wheat flour
1 cup soy okra
½ cup chick-pea flour
3 cups spinach, picked over, washed, and chopped
3 teaspoons salt (according to taste)
½ teaspoon turmeric powder
2 teaspoons chili powder (according to taste)
2 teaspoons fennel seeds
1 teaspoon cumin seeds
½ teaspoon garam masala
2 tablespoons chopped green pepper
About ½ cup water
pinch of asafetida
Soy oil for frying

1. Combine all the ingredients, except soy oil, in a bowl and mix well. Add enough water to make a dough.
2. Divide the dough into 10 to 12 equal portions and shape into round balls; if dough sticks, use a little oil. Sprinkle with a little flour; roll out on a lightly floured surface to 5-inch diameter.
3. Make palak paratha in the same manner as aloo paratha.
4. Serve warm with raita or chutney.

Suggestion: Make methi (fenugreek leaves) paratha in the same manner, substituting methi for palak.

Servings: 4   Time: 50 min.

Nutritional analysis per serving:

Calories	430	(RDA% 22)
Protein	12 gm	(RDA% 28)
Carbohydrate	60 gm	
Fat	16 gm	

Sweet Bread

Stuffed with Soybeans and Chick-Peas

Poran Poli

On the spring festival of colors called Holi, poran poli is baked in every household in India. Its sweet taste is tantalizing for my older son, who hides the poran poli in the refrigerator and enjoys it secretly for breakfast, lunch and dinner.

For dough

> 3 cups whole-wheat flour
> ½ teaspoon salt
> About 1⅓ cups water
> Butter for top

For filling

> 1 cup soybeans
> 2 cups chick-pea lentils
> 4½ cups sugar (according to taste)
> ½ teaspoon cardamom powder
> pinch of saffron (optional)
> Water as needed

1. Soak soybeans overnight or for 5 to 6 hours. Wash and boil them for 20 minutes. Again wash soybeans and chick-pea lentils, add 5 cups water, and boil in pressure cooker until soft. Discard all the water and blend to form a paste.

2. In a heavy pan put sugar, chick-pea lentils, and soybean paste and cook on low heat for ½ hour or until very thick. Keep stirring to prevent sticking. Add cardamom and saffron and let cool.

3. Combine all the ingredients for the dough in a bowl except butter. Add enough water to make a dough. Cover the bowl and set aside at room temperature for 20 minutes.

4. Knead the dough for 2 minutes; if it sticks, add ½ teaspoon butter. Divide dough into 22 to 24 equal portions and shape into balls. Sprinkle with a little flour and roll out each ball on a lightly floured surface to 4 inches in diameter. Place ¼ cup filling in the center of the circle and fold the edges over by pressing them together to enclose the filling. Press by hand and roll again to make a 5- to 6-inch circle. Roll carefully, so that the filling remains inside.

5. Heat a heavy skillet or frying pan and place one bread on the skillet. Cook for about ½ minute. With a wide spatula turn

bread over and grease the top with one teaspoon butter. Turn it over again and grease with one teaspoon butter and let it cook for about 1 minute. Fry for a few more minutes until both sides become golden.

6. Fry the other breads in the same manner. Each bread will take about 2 to 3 minutes to cook.

Servings: 8   Time: 120 min.

Nutritional analysis per serving:

Calories	687	(RDA% 34)
Protein	22 gm	(RDA% 49)
Carbohydrate	126 gm	
Fat	13 gm	

Soy Salads

THE SHORTCOMINGS OF traditional salads are that they can be boring in taste and barren in protein content. To change this we have introduced tofu and spices to salads, truly a unique combination. Tofu cubes of varying sizes can be added to the salad. Usually smaller cubes are better, because the added surface area allows the seasoning, spices and lemon juice to soak into the tofu. The pure white, bouncy tofu appears attractive on the leafy green salad.

One of our favorite recipes is the sweet and sour fruit salad, which combines various fruits into a tangy mixture. The mung and soy sprout salad has a fresh taste. Soy sprouts are made by soaking soybeans in water and placing them in a warm, dark place and allowing them to germinate. There are countless other salads; you can choose your favorite and make it tonight.

Cucumber, Tomato and Tofu Salad

Tomatoes and cucumbers are common ingredients in any salad. By adding tofu, these salads become hearty and nutritious.

½ cup finely chopped tofu
1 cup chopped cucumber
1 cup chopped tomato
2 hot green peppers, chopped
½ teaspoons salt (according to taste)
1 teaspoon cumin seeds
3 tablespoons chopped coriander leaves
1 teaspoon lemon juice

Mix all the ingredients. Serve cold.

Servings: 6   Time: 15 min.

Nutritional analysis per serving:

Calories	23	(RDA% 1)
Protein	2 gm	(RDA% 4)
Carbohydrate	3 gm	
Fat	1 gm	

Tomato and Tofu Salad

½ cup chopped tofu
2 cups chopped ripe tomatoes
½ cup chopped onion (optional)
1 tablespoon chopped hot green pepper
1 teaspoon lemon juice
1 teaspoon salt (according to taste)
1 teaspoon sugar
½ teaspoon cumin seeds
4 tablespoons chopped coriander leaves

Mix all the ingredients except coriander leaves. Garnish with coriander leaves and serve cold.

Servings: 6   Time: 15 min.

Nutritional analysis per serving:

Calories	31	(RDA% 2)
Protein	2 gm	(RDA% 5)
Carbohydrate	5 gm	
Fat	1 gm	

Coconut and Tofu Salad

Coconut is an unusual ingredient for salads; however, coconut and tofu salad is elegant in appearance and has a unique taste. It's fun for the daring cook.

1 cup freshly grated coconut
½ cup tofu, cut lengthwise
1 teaspoon salt (according to taste)
2 teaspoons hot peppers, chopped (optional)
6 curry leaves (optional)
1 teaspoon soy oil
½ teaspoon mustard seeds
1 tablespoon lemon juice
2 tablespoons chopped coriander leaves

1. Heat the soy oil in a frying pan, add mustard seeds, and fry for a few seconds. Add curry leaves and fry for 10 seconds.
2. Add all the other ingredients and mix. Serve cold.

Servings: 6   Time: 25 min.

Nutritional analysis per serving:

Calories	95	(RDA% 5)
Protein	2 gm	(RDA% 4)
Carbohydrate	8 gm	
Fat	7 gm	

Sweet-and-Sour Fruit Salad

Sweet-and-sour fruit salad is a mouth-watering dish and a sure success at any party.

¾ cup chopped tofu
1 cup peeled and chopped mango
1 ripe banana, chopped
2 medium-size tomatoes, chopped
1 medium-size apple, chopped
1 cup seedless grapes (cut in halves)
4 teaspoons sugar
2 teaspoons salt (according to taste)
1 teaspoon black pepper
1 tablespoon lemon juice
4 tablespoons chopped green pepper
3 tablespoons coriander leaves

Mix all the ingredients except coriander leaves. Garnish with coriander leaves and serve cold.

Servings: 4   Time: 20 min.

Nutritional analysis per serving:

Calories	241	(RDA% 12)
Protein	8 gm	(RDA% 17)
Carbohydrate	37 gm	
Fat	10 gm	

Cauliflower and Tofu Salad

2 cups cauliflower, chopped
1 cup tofu, chopped
2 teaspoons green pepper, chopped
½ cup onion, chopped
¼ cup chopped coriander leaves
1½ teaspoons salt (according to taste)
2 tablespoons lemon juice
1 teaspoon cumin seeds
2 carrots, cut in 1-inch pieces

1. Mix all the ingredients except carrots.
2. Put salad in the center of the serving plate and arrange the carrots all around. Serve cold.

Servings: 6   Time: 20 min.

Nutritional analysis per serving:

Calories	35	(RDA% 2)
Protein	3 gm	(RDA% 7)
Carbohydrate	3 gm	
Fat	1 gm	

Cucumber and Tofu Salad

½ cup finely chopped tofu
2 cups chopped cucumber
¼ cup chopped green pepper
2 hot peppers chopped (optional)
1½ teaspoons salt (according to taste)
1 teaspoon cumin seeds
3 tablespoons chopped coriander leaves
1 teaspoon lemon juice

Mix all the ingredients. Serve cold.

Servings: 6   Time: 15 min.

Nutritional analysis per serving:

Calories	19	(RDA% 1)
Protein	2 gm	(RDA% 3)
Carbohydrate	2 gm	
Fat	1 gm	

Radish and Tofu Salad

2 cups grated radishes
½ cup tofu, either grated or cut in small cubes
1 green pepper, chopped
2 teaspoons salt (according to taste)
1 cup chopped green coriander leaves
2 tomatoes, sliced (for decoration)
1 teaspoon cumin seeds
4 teaspoons lemon juice

1. Mix radishes and 1 teaspoon salt and set aside for 20 minutes. Then squeeze out all the water and mix with other ingredients, except tomatoes.
2. Place the radish and tofu salad in the center of a plate, and surround it with sliced tomatoes.

Servings: 10   Time: 20 min.

Nutritional analysis per serving:

Calories	13	(RDA% 1)
Protein	1 gm	(RDA% 2)
Carbohydrate	2 gm	
Fat	1 gm	

Spinach and Tofu Salad

1 cup chopped tofu
1 cup chopped radishes
2 cups chopped spinach
2 tomatoes, sliced (for decoration)
1 teaspoon salt (according to taste)
½ teaspoon ground red pepper
1 tablespoon lemon juice

1. Mix all the ingredients in a bowl, except tomato slices.
2. Spread in a serving plate and decorate with tomato slices. Serve cold.

Servings: 6   Time: 20 min.

Nutritional analysis per serving:

Calories	37	(RDA% 2)
Protein	3 gm	(RDA% 7)
Carbohydrate	4 gm	
Fat	1 gm	

Carrot and Tofu Salad

½ cup finely chopped tofu
2 cups grated carrots
2 green peppers, chopped
½ cup freshly grated coconut (optional)
4 curry leaves (optional)
2 teaspoons lemon juice
2 teaspoons salt (according to taste)
½ teaspoon mustard seeds
2 teaspoons soybean oil

1. Heat the oil in a frying pan, add mustard seeds, and fry for a few seconds. Add curry leaves and fry for 10 seconds.
2. Add all the other ingredients and mix. Cook for 1 minute. Serve cold.

Note: In the same way you can make unripe papaya salad.

Servings: 6   Time: 10 min.

Nutritional analysis per serving:

Calories	57	(RDA% 3)
Protein	2 gm	(RDA% 4)
Carbohydrate	8 gm	
Fat	2 gm	

Carrot Salad
With Soy Yogurt

Carrot salad with soy yogurt is a nutritious and colorful addition to a meal.

2 cups grated carrots
1 cup soy yogurt
2 teaspoons lemon juice
½ teaspoon chili powder (according to taste)
1 teaspoon salt (according to taste)
1 teaspoon cumin seeds, roasted and ground into powder
2 tablespoons chopped coriander leaves
1 teaspoon mustard seeds
2 teaspoons soy oil

1. In a small pan heat soy oil and fry mustard seeds for a few seconds.
2. Combine first six ingredients in a bowl. Add fried mustard seeds and oil on top. Decorate with coriander leaves. Serve cold.

Servings: 6   Time: 20 min.

Nutritional analysis per serving:

Calories	66	(RDA% 3)
Protein	3 gm	(RDA% 6)
Carbohydrate	9 gm	
Fat	3 gm	

Mung and Soy Sprouts Salad

Mung and soy sprouts salad is a fun way of enriching your diet with protein. It is easy to prepare and the entire family enjoys the fresh taste.

1 cup mung sprouts
1 cup soybean sprouts
1 cup chopped cucumber
½ cup chopped green pepper
2 tablespoons chopped hot green pepper
4 tablespoons chopped coriander leaves
2 tablespoons salt (according to taste)
1 teaspoon cumin seeds
2 tablespoons lemon juice
2 tomatoes, sliced for decoration
Few leaves of lettuce

1. Mix all the ingredients except tomato slices and lettuce leaves.
2. Place lettuce at the bottom of a serving plate. Spread the mixture over and surround with tomato slices. Serve cold.

How to grow sprouts:

1. Wash the soybeans and mung beans well. Soak them overnight in cold water.
2. Wash them in the morning and drain the water. Cover with nylon or cheesecloth over the top of the jar, secured with a ring or rubber band. Allow the seeds to sprout in a warm, dark place.
3. Wash the sprouts 2 to 3 times a day, and drain them thoroughly. Sprouts will be ready in 3 to 4 days. Wash them in cold water a few times and drain. Serve or store in an airtight container or plastic bag in the refrigerator. They will keep, refrigerated, for a few days.

Note: Mung and soybean sprouts are available in health food stores.

Servings: 8   Time: 15 min.

Nutritional analysis per serving:

Calories	21	(RDA% 1)
Protein	2 gm	(RDA% 4)
Carbohydrate	3 gm	
Fat	1 gm	

Soy Raitas and Chutney

A MEDIOCRE MEAL can become extraordinary with the quick preparation and addition of a raita or chutney. Both of these side dishes can be prepared from soybeans, soy yogurt, or tofu, making a highly nutritious complement to a meal.

Yogurt is a newcomer to the American diet; fruits with yogurt are a recent development, and for weight watchers a delightfully light and nutritious lunch. In India, yogurt, fruits, and vegetables are mixed to make a delicious dish called raita. Tofu and soy yogurt can be substituted, or accompanied with cow's milk yogurt to make a highly nutritious dish. Both yogurts and tofu create a setting of mild, smooth taste that enhances the flavor of your favorite vegetable.

Raitas are eaten with chappati or rice. You can dip in a piece of aloo paratha, bread stuffed with potatoes and tofu, or you can mix the raita with navaratan pulav, a colorful rice.

Chutneys are a miniaturized version of sauces. Their sole purpose is to add aroma, texture and spice to the meal. Often chutney is a test which separates an amateur cook from a chef. Though it is difficult to decide the perfect mix of spices for your guests' sensitive palates, chutney is very easy to prepare. Once you pull together all the ingredients, the blender does the rest.

Chutney can be prepared quickly and stored in the refrigerator. During the week it can be used as a spread in place of mayonnaise or as a dip with afternoon snacks or appetizers.

An additional advantage of both chutney and raita is that they can be prepared well before serving, hence you are not rushed while preparing your main course.

127

Spinach and Tofu Raita

Palak tofu raita is a nutritionist's delight. Spinach—high in iron and vitamins; and tofu—high in protein, make a great side dish when combined.

1 cup boiled spinach
1 cup plain yogurt
1 cup tofu
1 teaspoon roasted ground cumin seeds
½ teaspoon red pepper (according to taste)
1½ teaspoons salt (according to taste)
2 teaspoons lemon juice

Blend spinach and tofu. Add yogurt and all the other ingredients and blend until smooth. Chill the raita before serving.

Note: You can replace tofu with soy yogurt.

Servings: 8   Time: 20 min.

Nutritional analysis per serving:

Calories	25	(RDA% 2)
Protein	3 gm	(RDA% 7)
Carbohydrate	2 gm	
Fat	2 gm	

Potato and Tofu Raita

For potato lovers, potato tofu raita is wonderful—spicy in flavor, easy to make.

1 cup potatoes boiled, peeled, and diced
2 cups plain yogurt
½ cup chopped tofu
½ teaspoon chili powder (according to taste)
1½ teaspoons salt (according to taste)
1 teaspoon roasted and blended cumin seeds
2 tablespoons chopped coriander leaves

1. Whisk the yogurt to a smooth paste. Combine all the ingredients except coriander leaves and mix well.
2. Garnish with coriander leaves. Cover and refrigerate until ready to serve.

Servings: 6   Time: 15 min.

Nutritional analysis per serving:

Calories	87	(RDA% 4)
Protein	5 gm	(RDA% 10)
Carbohydrate	11 gm	
Fat	3 gm	

Carrot, Zucchini, and Raisin Raita

With Tofu

If you are having trouble deciding between a sweet or spicy raita, try carrot, zucchini and raisin raita with tofu. It has a spicy red chili taste and a sweet raisin taste, as well as a mixture of vegetables. It is sure to tickle the palate.

2 cups plain yogurt
½ cup mashed tofu
1 green squash, shredded
1 carrot, shredded
¼ cup raisins soaked in warm water
2 teaspoons salt (according to taste)
½ teaspoon chili powder (according to taste)
½ teaspoon roasted cumin seeds
2 tablespoons coriander leaves

1. Whisk the yogurt into a smooth paste. Mix all the ingredients except coriander leaves.
2. Garnish with coriander leaves. Cover and refrigerate until ready to serve.

Servings: 6   Time: 15 min.

Nutritional analysis per serving:

Calories	84	(RDA% 4)
Protein	4 gm	(RDA% 10)
Carbohydrate	11 gm	
Fat	3 gm	

Cucumber Raita

1 cup soy yogurt
1 cup plain yogurt
1 cup grated cucumber
2 tablespoons chopped fresh mint
½ teaspoon chili powder (according to taste)
1 teaspoon salt (according to taste)
1 teaspoon roasted and blended cumin seeds

Whisk the yogurt into a smooth paste. Add all ingredients and mix well. Cover and refrigerate until ready to serve.

Servings: 6   Time: 20 min.

Nutritional analysis per serving:

Calories	49	(RDA% 2)
Protein	3 gm	(RDA% 7)
Carbohydrate	5 gm	
Fat	2 gm	

Tomato Raita

2 medium-size ripe tomatoes, chopped
1 cup soy yogurt
1 cup plain yogurt
1½ teaspoons salt (according to taste)
½ teaspoon chili powder (according to taste)
½ teaspoon mustard seeds
1 tablespoon soy oil
3 tablespoons chopped green coriander leaves

1. Whisk yogurt into a smooth paste. Add tomatoes, salt and chili powder.
2. In a small frying pan heat the oil and add the mustard seeds. When the mustard seeds start popping, pour the seasoning over the yogurt mixture. Stir carefully to mix the ingredients.
3. Garnish with coriander leaves. Keep in refrigerator; serve cold.

Servings: 6   Time: 15 min.

Nutritional analysis per serving:

Calories	72	(RDA% 4)
Protein	3 gm	(RDA% 8)
Carbohydrate	5 gm	
Fat	5 gm	

Pumpkin Raita

1 cup pumpkin, grated or chopped small
1 cup plain yogurt
1 cup soy yogurt
½ teaspoon chili powder (according to taste)
1½ teaspoons salt (according to taste)
½ teaspoon roasted and blended cumin seeds
3 tablespoons chopped coriander leaves

1. Boil the pumpkin for about 10 minutes. Drain and let it cool.
2. Whisk yogurt into a paste. Add all the ingredients except coriander leaves and mix well.
3. Garnish with coriander leaves. Refrigerate until ready to serve.

Squash raita can be made by substituting squash for pumpkin.

Servings: 6   Time: 15 min.

Nutritional analysis per serving:

Calories	46	(RDA% 2)
Protein	3 gm	(RDA% 7)
Carbohydrate	4 gm	
Fat	2 gm	

Sweet Banana Raita

For my older son, who has a sweet tooth, we frequently make banana raita with sweet soy yogurt. Its sweet taste is enhanced by the fragrance of cardamom and saffron.

1 cup soy yogurt
1 cup plain yogurt
2 tablespoons raisins
¼ teaspoon cardamom powder
2 teaspoons chopped almonds and pistachio nuts
½ cup sugar
2 ripe bananas, thinly sliced
pinch of saffron

1. Soak raisins in 1 cup warm water for about 20 minutes. Discard all the water from the raisins. Soak saffron in 1 teaspoon milk or warm water. Blend the saffron by finger or spoon.

2. Whisk yogurt into a paste and add all the ingredients. Chill before serving.

Servings: 6   Time: 15 min.

Nutritional analysis per serving:

Calories	92	(RDA% 5)
Protein	4 gm	(RDA% 8)
Carbohydrate	16 gm	
Fat	2 gm	

Soy Flour Pearls Raita
Bundi Raita

Appearing like pearls in a sea of yogurt, soy flour pearls raita is an alluring and nutritious side dish.

   1 cup soy flour pearls
   1 cup plain yogurt
   1 cup soy yogurt and 1 cup plain yogurt
   ½ teaspoon red pepper (according to taste)
   1½ teaspoons salt (according to taste)
   ½ teaspoon roasted and blended cumin seeds
   2 tablespoons chopped coriander leaves

1. Prepare soy flour pearls (see recipe in soy dessert section).
2. Soak soy flour pearls in warm water for about half an hour. Softly squeeze pearls between the palms and strain off the water.
3. Whisk the yogurt into a paste. Add all the ingredients except coriander leaves and mix well.
4. Garnish with coriander leaves. Cover and refrigerate until ready to serve.

Servings: 6   Time: 30 min.

Nutritional analysis per serving:
   Calories   113   (RDA% 6)
   Protein   7 gm   (RDA% 16)
   Carbohydrate   15 gm
   Fat   3 gm

Soybean Chutney

Several varieties of soybean chutney are presented. All are very nutritious.

¼ cup dry soybeans (or ¾ cup soaked soybeans)
1½ teaspoons salt (according to taste)
1 teaspoon chili powder (according to taste)
2 tablespoons ginger, chopped
5 tablespoons lemon juice

1. Soak dry soybeans overnight or for 6 to 8 hours.
2. Wash and boil soaked soybeans for about 10 minutes.
3. Add all the other ingredients and blend into a paste by adding a little water.
4. Serve cold with idli or pakoras.

Servings: 6   Time: 20 min.

Nutritional analysis per serving:

Calories	41	(RDA% 2)
Protein	4 gm	(RDA% 9)
Carbohydrate	2 gm	
Fat	2 gm	

Tomato Chutney

2 large ripe tomatoes
¼ cup tofu
5 green chilies (according to taste)
1½ teaspoons salt (according to taste)
½ teaspoon cumin seeds
3 tablespoons lemon juice
1 tablespoon chopped ginger
Pinch of asafeetida
1 Onion (optional)

Combine all the ingredients and blend until the tomatoes turn into a paste. Refrigerate until ready to serve.

Servings: 8   Time: 10 min.

Nutritional analysis per serving:

Calories	11	(RDA% 1)
Protein	1 gm	(RDA% 2)
Carbohydrate	2 gm	
Fat	0 gm	

Unripe Mango Chutney

2 unripe mangoes, peeled and sliced
⅓ cup tofu
1 teaspoon salt
2 tablespoons sugar (optional)
5 green hot chilies
½-inch piece of ginger root
1 teaspoon cumin seeds
1 cup green coriander leaves

Combine all the ingredients and blend into a creamy paste. Add a little water if needed. Refrigerate until ready to serve.

Servings: 10   Time: 15 min.

Nutritional analysis per serving:

Calories	41	(RDA% 2)
Protein	1 gm	(RDA% 2)
Carbohydrate	10 gm	
Fat	1 gm	

Coriander Tofu Chutney

3 cups chopped fresh coriander leaves
½ cup tofu
5 hot green chilies (according to taste)
1 teaspoon salt (according to taste)
1 teaspoon cumin seeds
6 tablespoons lemon juice
2 tablespoons ginger, chopped
Pinch of asafetida

Combine all the ingredients and blend into a paste. Pour the chutney into a jar, and keep in the refrigerator until ready to serve. Mint chutney can be made by substituting mint for coriander.

Servings: 8   Time: 10 min.

Nutritional analysis per serving:

Calories	13	(RDA% 1)
Protein	1 gm	(RDA% 2)
Carbohydrate	2 gm	
Fat	0 gm	

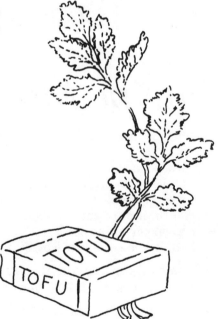

Coriander Soybean Chutney

¼ cup dry soybeans (or ¾ cup soaked soybeans)
1 cup chopped coriander leaves
6 hot green peppers (according to taste)
1½ teaspoons salt (according to taste)
1 teaspoon cumin seeds
2 tablespoons ginger, chopped
5 tablespoons lemon juice

1. Soak dry soybeans overnight or for 6 to 8 hours.
2. Wash and boil soaked soybeans for about 10 minutes.
3. Add all the ingredients and blend into a paste by adding a little water.
4. Serve cold with idli or pakoras.

Servings: 8   Time: 20 min.

Nutritional analysis per serving:

Calories	55	(RDA% 3)
Protein	5 gm	(RDA% 10)
Carbohydrate	2 gm	
Fat	2 gm	

Coconut Soybean Chutney

Our favorite is coconut soybean chutney. It has a nutty taste, a rough coconut texture, and a tropical aromatic fragrance, all of which combine to give sensuous pleasure to a meal.

¼ cup dry soybeans (or ¾ cup soaked soybeans)
½ cup fresh coconut, peeled and chopped
2 tablespoons ginger, chopped
4 green chilies
1 teaspoon salt (according to taste)
1 teaspoon cumin seeds
5 tablespoons lemon juice

Combine all the ingredients and blend into a creamy paste. Refrigerate until ready to serve.

Servings: 10   Time: 10 min.

Nutritional analysis per serving:

Calories	71	(RDA% 4)
Protein	3 gm	(RDA% 6)
Carbohydrate	6 gm	
Fat	4 gm	

Radish Chutney

1 cup white radishes, peeled and cut
¼ cup tofu
2 green chilies
½-inch piece of ginger root
2½ tablespoons lemon juice
1 teaspoon salt

Combine all the ingredients and blend into a creamy paste. Refrigerate until ready to serve.

Servings: 10   Time: 10 min.

Nutritional analysis per serving:

Calories	10	(RDA% 1)
Protein	1 gm	(RDA% 2)
Carbohydrate	1 gm	
Fat	0 gm	

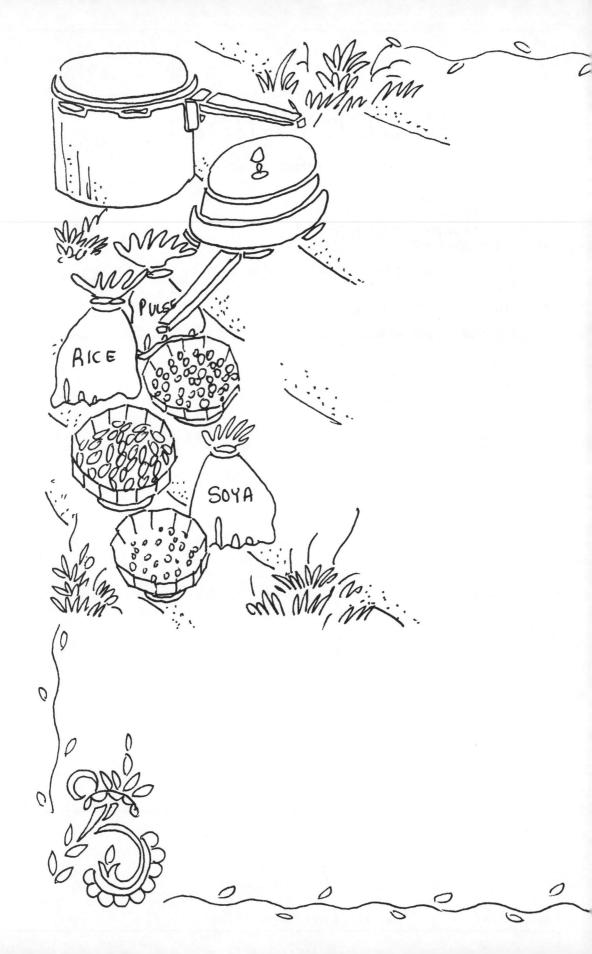

Soy, Rice and Lentils

RICE, A SYMBOL OF prosperity and fertility in the East, is the staple food for half the world's population. The Western diet has unfortunately ignored this complex carbohydrate and has only treated it as a side dish. The wonder of this food is that it can be served as part of any meal.

Rice dishes can be prepared in several ways. Rice with soy okra or tofu with rice are simple recipes, which are to be accompanied by lentils, raita or soy vegetables. Extravagant rice preparations are rice mixed with spices. Our favorite is matar paneer pulav, rice with peas and tofu, and navaratan pulav, colorful rice, which is tasty as well as attractive.

Chaval and dal, rice and lentils, go together to make a main course. They complement each other not only in taste but in texture and appearance. The white fluffy rice integrates well with either a yellow or a dark curried soy lentils or mung lentils. Even more impressive about this dual food combination is the protein complementation that occurs. The low amount of lysine and high quantity of cystine and methionine found in rice is complemented by the high amounts of lysine and low amounts of cystine and methionine found in soy foods such as tofu, okra, soy lentils and other lentils. This can boost the usable protein content of a meal by 40 percent. Like a key fitting into a lock, these two foods combine to open the door to a new repertoire of nutritious vegetarian recipes.

You need not make this nutritious combination of rice and soy dal or lentils in separate dishes. When made in combination, it is called khichadi. Tofu and spices can be added to rice and soy lentils to make a highly nutritious and delightfully tasty one food meal, tofu khichadi.

Lentils hold a very special place in the Indian menu. They are a must at every meal, just as bread is, and are a major source of protein for the vegetarian diet.

Soy lentils, soy dal, is highly nutritious and very appetizing. It is made simply by soaking, dehulling, and splitting the soybeans. Lentil recipes such as mung lentils with spinach and okra, toovar lentils with soy lentils, or five-lentil soup are delightful. However, the king of all the lentil recipes is soybean sambhar, soybean and lentils with vegetables.

141

Rice with Soy Okra

For many years we ate plain rice, but now we have discovered rice with soy okra, which provides more fiber than oatmeal. It is best enjoyed with lentil soup.

  2 cups basmati or plain rice
  1 cup soy okra
  2 teaspoons salt (according to taste)
  4 cups water

1. Wash rice if basmati rice is used. Then soak the rice for 2 hours.
2. Drain the rice and put in a pan. Add 4 cups of water, soy okra, and salt, then cook on high heat until the rice starts boiling. Let it boil about 2 minutes. Turn the heat to medium-low, stir the rice, cover, and cook on low heat for 10 to 15 minutes, or until done. Serve hot.

Servings: 8   Time: 40 min.

Nutritional analysis per serving:

Calories	62	(RDA% 3)
Protein	2 gm	(RDA% 4)
Carbohydrate	12 gm	
Fat	1 gm	

Tofu Rice

Many people serve plain rice, but now, by adding tofu and cinnamon, you can increase the nutritive value of the rice as well as create a tasty, aromatic side dish.

2 cups basmati or plain rice
1 cup mashed or chopped tofu
1 teaspoon salt (according to taste)
2 tablespoons soy oil
1 teaspoon cumin seeds
2 sticks cinnamon
4 cups water

1. Wash rice if basmati rice is used. Then soak the rice for 1 to 2 hours.
2. Heat soy oil in a pan. Add cumin seeds and cinnamon sticks and fry for a few seconds, then add tofu and fry for 3 to 4 minutes.
3. Drain rice, add to the pan and fry on medium heat for 5 to 6 minutes. Add 4 cups water and cook on high heat until rice starts to boil. Let boil for 2 minutes. Lower heat to medium-low, stir the rice, cover, and cook for 10 to 15 minutes, or until done.
4. Serve warm with lentils or curry.

Servings: 8   Time: 30 min.

Nutritional analysis per serving:

Calories	90	(RDA% 4)
Protein	3 gm	(RDA% 6)
Carbohydrate	10 gm	
Fat	5 gm	

Rice with Peas and Tofu

Matar Paneer Pulav

When friends come over for a get-together, rice with peas and tofu is an easy but elegant rice preparation. This dish in combination with any soy raita can also serve as a light meal.

1½ cups plain or basmati rice
1 cup peas
1½ cups fried tofu cubes
2½ teaspoons salt (according to taste)
1 teaspoon chili powder
½ teaspoon turmeric powder
About 3 cups water

For seasoning (tarka)

3 tablespoons soy oil
½ teaspoon cumin seeds
½ teaspoon mustard seeds
2 bay leaves
Pinch of asafetida

For decoration

½ teaspoon garam masala
2 tablespoons chopped coriander leaves

1. Wash rice if basmati rice is used. Then soak for 2 to 3 hours. Heat the soy oil in a heavy pan. Add all the seasonings and fry for a few seconds. Drain the rice and add to pan. Fry rice for 3 to 4 minutes.

2. Add peas, tofu and all the spices. Mix thoroughly and fry for about 2 minutes. Add 3 cups of water and cook over high heat until the rice starts to boil. Let boil for 2 minutes. Lower heat to medium-low, stir the rice, cover, and cook on low heat for about 10 to 15 minutes or until done.

3. Add garam masala. Garnish with coriander leaves, and serve warm.

Servings: 6   Time: 45 min.

Nutritional analysis per serving:

Calories	157	(RDA% 8)
Protein	6 gm	(RDA% 13)
Carbohydrate	14 gm	
Fat	9 gm	

Soy Yogurt Rice
Soy Dahi Rice

My two-year-old granddaughter loves soy dahi rice and could eat it at every meal. The sight of her small face all covered with soy yogurt makes us laugh.

1 cup rice
½ cup soy yogurt
½ cup plain yogurt
1 teaspoon chili powder
1½ teaspoons salt (according to taste)
2 cups water

For seasoning (tarka)

½ teaspoon mustard seeds
½ teaspoon cumin seeds
2 whole red peppers
2 tablespoons soy oil
Pinch of asafetida

For decoration

1 teaspoon chopped ginger
3 tablespoons coriander leaves
1 tablespoon chopped green pepper

1. Wash rice if basmati rice is used. Then soak the rice for 2 to 3 hours. In a heavy pan boil 4 cups water. Drain the rice and add to the boiling water. Cook at medium heat for 5 minutes, then stir and turn to low heat. Let it simmer for 15 minutes, or until done.

2. Mix plain and soy yogurt, salt and chili powder in the rice. In a heavy pan heat soy oil. Add all the seasonings in it, and fry for a few seconds. Add mixed rice in the seasonings and stir properly. Cook at low heat for 2 minutes.

3. Remove to a serving plate. Garnish with decorations. Serve warm.

Servings: 4   Time: 45 min.

Nutritional analysis per serving

Calories	114	(RDA% 6)
Protein	2 gm	(RDA% 3)
Carbohydrate	16 gm	
Fat	4 gm	

Colorful Rice
Navaratan Pulav

When served in a clear glass dish, the white, green, and pink colors of navaratan pulav are sure to raise your guests' eyebrows, and you will get requests for the recipe.

2½ cups basmati or plain rice
1½ cups mashed tofu
2 teaspoons salt (according to taste)
5 cups water

For seasoning (tarka)

3 tablespoons soy oil
½ teaspoon cumin seeds
¼ cup cashew nuts
¼ cup raisins

For decoration

1 cup boiled peas
3 tablespoons chopped coriander
4 tablespoons chopped green pepper
green food coloring
red food coloring
½ teaspoon chili powder (according to taste)

1. Wash rice if basmati rice is used. Then soak the rice for 2 to 3 hours. In a heavy pan boil 5 cups water and salt. Drain the rice, and add to boiling water; let it cook for 5 minutes. Stir and turn to low heat. Add tofu and mix well. Simmer for 15 minutes or until done.

2. In a small pan heat soy oil and fry cumin seeds. Add cashew nuts and raisins and fry for a few seconds.

3. Divide the rice in three parts. Set one portion aside. In two tablespoons of warm water add a few drops of red food coloring, and mix it into the second portion of the rice.

4. Take two tablespoons warm water and add a few drops of green food coloring. Mix one cup of boiled peas, coriander leaves, chopped green pepper, and green coloring into the third portion of rice, and mix well.

5. In a glass dish, spread the portion of white rice, then spread the portion of green rice, and then the portion of pink rice. Now spread the nut and raisin mixture over it. Serve warm.

Servings: 10   Time: 45 min.

Nutritional analysis per serving:

Calories	260	(RDA% 13)
Protein	6 gm	(RDA% 14)
Carbohydrate	46 gm	
Fat	6 gm	

Rice with Lentils
Plain Khichadi

A combination of rice and lentils is called khichadi.

1½ cups rice
½ cup soy lentils
¼ cup mung lentils
2 teaspoons salt
7 cups water (approximately)
½ teaspoon turmeric powder

1. Wash rice (if basmati rice is used), soy lentils and mung lentils separately. In a heavy pan boil water, add soy lentils and boil for 20 minutes. Then add rice and mung lentils. Cover and cook slowly for 30 to 40 minutes, or until lentils and rice are done. Add more water if needed. Stir occasionally to prevent khichadi from sticking.
2. Add salt and turmeric powder and mix properly. Serve warm with butter.

Servings: 6   Time: 60 min.

Nutritional analysis per serving:

Calories	267	(RDA% 13)
Protein	12 gm	(RDA% 28)
Carbohydrate	44 gm	
Fat	4 gm	

Tofu with Rice and Lentils
Tofu Khichadi

A quick lunch preparation is tofu with rice and lentils. It is a light meal enjoyed by all.

1½ cups rice
1 cup mung lentils
½ teaspoon turmeric powder
2 teaspoons salt (according to taste)
About 7 to 8 cups water

For seasoning (tarka)

4 tablespoons soy oil
½ teaspoon cumin seeds
1 teaspoon mustard seeds
Pinch of asafetida

Spices and vegetables

1 large onion, chopped
1½ cups mashed tofu
2 large tomatoes, chopped
1 cup boiled peas (optional)
1 teaspoon chili powder (according to taste)
½ teaspoon garam masala

For decoration

2 tablespoons chopped green pepper
3 tablespoons chopped coriander leaves
2 tablespoons chopped ginger

1. Wash rice (if basmati rice is used) and mung lentils. In a heavy pan add rice, mung lentils, salt, turmeric powder, and 6 cups of water. Cover and cook slowly for 40 to 50 minutes, or until lentils and rice are done. Add more water if needed. Stir occasionally to prevent khichadi from sticking.
2. In a small pan heat soy oil. Add seasoning and fry for a few seconds. Add onion and fry until it turns light brown. Add tofu and fry for 3 to 4 minutes. Add tomatoes, boiled peas, and all the spices and cook until oil starts oozing out. Add this to khichadi and mix well.

4. Garnish with coriander leaves, green pepper and chopped ginger and serve warm.

Servings: 6   Time: 60 min.

Nutritional analysis per serving:

Calories	383	(RDA% 19)
Protein	13 gm	(RDA% 30)
Carbohydrate	57 gm	
Fat	12 gm	

Mung Lentils
With Spinach and Soy Okra

Mung is one of the favorite lentils of India. In combination with soy okra and spinach it makes a hearty soup, enjoyed with soy bread or rice.

1 cup soybean okra
1 cup mung lentils
2 cups fresh spinach, chopped
1 cup tomatoes, chopped
1 teaspoon chili powder (according to taste)
3 teaspoons salt (according to tste)
½ teaspoon turmeric powder
½ teaspoon garam masala
½ teaspoon cumin seeds
1 tablespoon ginger, chopped
3 cloves
3 tablespoons soy oil
Pinch of asafetida
About 8 cups water

1. Wash the lentils and add 6 cups water, soy okra, spinach, salt, and turmeric powder. Cook in a pressure cooker or in a deep pot until lentils become tender. Add 1 to 2 cups water, mix well, and cook for a few more minutes.

2. Heat soy oil and add cumin seeds, cloves and asafetida. After a few seconds add chopped ginger, tomatoes, and all the other spices. Cook for 3 to 4 minutes, then mix into lentils. Serve warm with rice or bread.

Servings: 8   Time: 50 min.

Nutritional analysis per serving:

Calories	139	(RDA% 7)
Protein	9 gm	(RDA% 19)
Carbohydrate	21 gm	
Fat	3 gm	

Fried Rice and Lentils
Bhooni Khichadi

1½ cups rice
½ cup soy lentils
½ cup toovar lentils
1 teaspoon chili powder
2 teaspoons salt
½ teaspoon turmeric powder
½ teaspoon garam masala

For seasoning (tarka)

3 tablespoons soy oil
½ teaspoon cumin seeds
½ teaspoon mustard seeds
2 sticks of cinnamon
4 cloves
Pinch of asafetida

For decoration

1 teaspoon chopped ginger
1 tablespoon chopped green chili
3 tablespoons green coriander leaves
2 large tomatoes, chopped

1. Soak soy lentils for 4 to 5 hours and then boil for 20 minutes. Wash the soy lentils, toovar lentils, and rice (if basmati rice is used).
2. Heat soy oil in a heavy pan, add seasoning and fry for a few seconds. Drain the soy lentils and toovar lentils, add to seasoning, and fry for 5 to 6 minutes.
3. Add all the spices except garam masala and mix well. Add 6 cups warm water, cover, and cook on medium-low heat for 30 to 40 minutes. Stir to prevent sticking.
4. When cooked, add garam masala and mix well. Garnish with coriander leaves, green chili, ginger and tomatoes. Serve warm.

Servings: 8   Time: 60 min.

Nutritional analysis per serving:

Calories	281	(RDA% 14)
Protein	12 gm	(RDA% 27)
Carbohydrate	39 gm	
Fat	8 gm	

Black Soybean Curry

Black soybeans are difficult to find even in health-food stores, yet when found they make a delightful curry.

1 cup black soybeans
½ teaspoon baking soda (optional)
About 6 cups water for boiling

For sauce

2 fresh tomatoes, chopped
1 large chopped onion (optional)
1 tablespoon chopped fresh ginger
2 teaspoons chopped green chili
1 teaspoon chili powder (according to taste)
1½ teaspoons salt (according to taste)
½ teaspoon turmeric powder
2 teaspoons coriander powder
1 teaspoon mango powder (amchur)

For seasoning (tarka)

3 tablespoons soy oil
½ teaspoon cumin seeds
Pinch of asafetida

For decoration

½ teaspoon garam masala
4 tablespoons chopped green coriander leaves
1 tomato, sliced

1. Soak black soybeans overnight or for 6 to 8 hours. Wash them, add baking soda and 6 cups of water, and boil until they become tender. (Use pressure cooker for quick cooking.)
2. Blend all sauce ingredients into a paste.
3. Heat soy oil, add seasoning, and fry for a few seconds. Add all the paste and cook until oil starts oozing out. Add paste to the beans and mix well. Cook for 4 to 5 minutes.
4. Sprinkle with garam masala, then garnish with coriander leaves and tomato slices. Serve with rice.

Servings: 6   Time: 60 min.

Nutritional analysis per serving:

Calories	242	(RDA% 12)
Protein	17 gm	(RDA% 39)
Carbohydrate	12 gm	
Fat	14 gm	

Fried Mung Lentils

With Tofu

Our family's favorite lentil dish with an evening meal.

1 cup mung lentils
½ cup tofu
1 tomato, chopped
1 teaspoon chili powder (according to taste)
2½ teaspoons salt (according to taste)
2 teaspoons coriander powder
½ teaspoon turmeric powder
2 teaspoons mango powder (amchur)
About 2 cups water

For seasoning (tarka)

½ teaspoon cumin seeds
3 tablespoons soy oil
Pinch of asafetida

For decoration

2 tablespoons coriander leaves
2 teaspoons chopped green pepper
2 teaspooons chopped ginger
¼ teaspoon garam masala

1. Wash and soak the mung lentils in water overnight, or for 4 to 5 hours.
2. In a heavy pan heat the soy oil, add all the seasoning, and fry for a few seconds. Add chopped tofu and fry for 2 to 3 minutes or until tofu turns light brown. Add chopped tomato and cook for 4 to 5 minutes.
3. Add all the spices, fry for a minute, then add mung lentils. Mix well, then add 1½ cups water, cover, and cook on low heat until lentils become tender but not overcooked. If needed, add more water.
4. Add garam masala. Garnish with coriander leaves and chopped green pepper. Serve with rice or bread.

Servings: 6   Time: 30 min.

Nutritional analysis per serving:

Calories	202	(RDA% 10)
Protein	11 gm	(RDA% 24)
Carbohydrate	23 gm	
Fat	8 gm	

Fried Soy Lentils

Fried soy lentils is a completely new creation in the repertoire of lentil recipes. It measures up to the taste of all the other lentil dishes.

1 cup soy lentils
½ teaspoon baking soda (optional)
About 6 cups water

For sauce

2 large tomatoes, chopped
1 large chopped onion (optional)
1 tablespoon chopped fresh ginger
½ teaspoon chili powder (according to taste)
2 teaspoons coriander powder
2 teaspoons salt (according to taste)
½ teaspoon turmeric powder

For seasoning (tarka)

1 bay leaf
3 tablespoons soy oil
½ teaspoon cumin seeds
Pinch of asafetida

For decoration

½ teaspoon garam masala
2 teaspoons mango powder (amchur)
2 tablespoons chopped coriander leaves

1. Soak soy lentils overnight or for 6 to 8 hours. Wash, add ½ teaspoon baking soda, then boil for 30 minutes or until tender.
2. Blend all the ingredients for sauce into a paste.
3. Heat soy oil, add seasoning, and fry for a few seconds. Add all the paste and cook until oil starts oozing out. Add 1 cup water and soy lentils to the paste and cook for 10 minutes.
4. Mix in mango powder, sprinkle with garam masala, and garnish with coriander leaves. Serve warm with rice.

Servings: 6   Time: 60 min.

Nutritional analysis per serving:

Calories	242	(RDA% 12)
Protein	17 gm	(RDA% 39)
Carbohydrate	12 gm	
Fat	14 gm	

Dried Pigeon Peas

With Soy Lentils

Toovar Dal With Soy Dal

Toovar lentils are the most frequently used variety of lentils in the Indian home. The addition of soy makes it a nutritious dish.

1 cup toovar lentils
½ cup soy lentils
1 teaspoon chili powder
½ teaspoon paprika (optional)
2½ teaspoons salt (according to taste)
½ teaspoon turmeric powder
4 tablespoons soy oil
½ teaspoon cumin seeds
2 teaspoons chopped ginger root
2 tablespoons chopped coriander leaves
2 teaspoons chopped green pepper
pinch of asafetida
pinch of baking soda (optional)
about 5 cups water

1. Wash soy lentils and soak for 3 to 4 hours (otherwise boil for 20 minutes). Wash toovar lentils, mix in soy lentils, add 4 to 5 cups water and baking soda, and cook in a pressure cooker until tender.

2. Add salt and turmeric powder and mix well. If needed, add more water.

3. In a small pan heat soy oil. Add asafetida and cumin seeds and fry them for a few seconds. Add the remaining ingredients, except for the coriander leaves, and blend into the lentils. Decorate with coriander leaves and serve with rice or bread.

Note: Soy okra may be substituted for the soy lentils.

Servings: 6   Time: 50 min.

Nutritional analysis per serving:

Calories	292	(RDA% 15)
Protein	18 gm	(RDA% 40)
Carbohydrate	26 gm	
Fat	13 gm	

Spicy Lentils
With Tofu
Masala Masoor with Tofu

1 cup whole masoor lentils
½ cup chopped tofu

Grind to a paste (for the sauce)

2 chopped tomatoes
1 onion (optional)
1 teaspoon chili powder (according to taste)
2 teaspoons salt (according to taste)
3 teaspoons coriander powder
½ teaspoon turmeric powder
1 teaspoon cumin seeds
1 tablespoon ginger, chopped
about 6 to 8 cups water

For seasoning (tarka)

3 tablespoons soy oil
½ teaspoon cumin seeds
pinch of asafetida

For decoration

½ teaspoon garam masala
4 tablespoons chopped green coriander leaves
1 tablespoon chopped green pepper

1. Wash the masoor lentils, add 4 cups water, and cook until tender (about 40 to 50 minutes). Add water as needed.
2. Heat soy oil, add seasoning, and fry for a few seconds. Add tofu and fry for 4 to 5 minutes, until tofu becomes a little brown. Add the paste and cook until oil starts oozing out. Add paste to the lentils and mix properly. Cook for 4 to 5 minutes.
3. Sprinkle with garam masala, and garnish with coriander leaves and green pepper. Serve warm with rice or bread.

Servings: 6   Time: 50 min.

Nutritional analysis per serving:

Calories	220	(RDA% 11)
Protein	12 gm	(RDA% 26)
Carbohydrate	27 gm	
Fat	8 gm	

Five-Lentil Soup
Panch Mel

Here all kinds of lentils are combined to make a rich-tasting soup.

½ cup soy lentils
½ cup toovar lentils (dried pigeon peas)
¼ cup urad lentils (black gram dal)
¼ cup chick-pea lentils
¼ cup mung lentils

Grind into a paste (for the sauce)

2 tomatoes, chopped (optional)
½ cup chopped onion
2 teaspoons chopped ginger
2 teaspoons chili powder (according to taste)
2 teaspoons salt (according to taste)
2 teaspoons coriander powder
½ teaspoon turmeric powder
about 6 to 7 cups water

For seasoning (tarka)

4 tablespoons soy oil
½ teaspoon cumin seeds
2 bay leaves
pinch of asafetida

For decoration

½ teaspoon garam masala
2 teaspoons mango powder (amchur)
4 teaspoons chopped green coriander leaves
2 tablespoons lemon juice (according to taste)

1. Wash and soak soy lentils for 3 to 4 hours in warm water (or cook for 30 minutes). Wash all the lentils and mix them together.
2. Put water in a heavy pan, add the lentils, and cook for 40 to 60 minutes on low heat, until they are tender and well-mixed. Add salt and turmeric and mix well. Cook again for 20 minutes.
3. In a heavy pan heat soy oil, add all the seasoning ingredients and fry for a few seconds. Add all the paste and cook until oil starts oozing out. Add lentils to the paste and mix well.

4. Mix in mango powder and lemon juice. Sprinkle with garam masala and garnish with coriander leaves. Serve warm with rice or bread.

Servings: 8   Time: 70 min.

Nutritional analysis per serving:

Calories	251	(RDA% 13)
Protein	15 gm	(RDA% 35)
Carbohydrate	25 gm	
Fat	10 gm	

Soy Lentils

With Cucumbers

¼ cup soy lentils
¼ cup chick-pea lentils
3 cups chopped cucumbers
½ teaspoon chili powder (according to taste)
2 teaspoons salt (according to taste)
½ teaspoon turmeric powder
1 teaspoon coriander powder
½ teaspoon garam masala
1½ teaspoons mango powder (amchur)
2 teaspoons chopped ginger
2 teaspoons chopped green pepper
3 tablespoons chopped green coriander leaves
3 tablespoons soy oil
½ teaspoon cumin seeds
pinch of asafetida
pinch of baking soda (optional)
about 4 cups water

1. Soak soy lentils and chick-pea lentils separately overnight. Wash them well.
2. In a heavy pan heat soy oil, add cumin seeds and asafetida. Fry for a few seconds, then add chili powder, turmeric powder and soy lentils. Mix well, add 2 cups water and baking soda and cook for 20 minutes.
3. Add chick-pea lentils, chopped cucumbers and salt and cook for 25 minutes, or until lentils are tender. Add 1 cup water and all the spices except coriander leaves. Cook for 2 to 3 minutes.
4. Place in a serving dish and garnish with coriander leaves.

Servings: 6   Time: 30 min.

Nutritional analysis per serving:

Calories	146	(RDA% 7)
Protein	6 gm	(RDA% 14)
Carbohydrate	10 gm	
Fat	9 gm	

Black Gram Lentils

With Tofu

Urad Dal with Tofu

1 cup black gram lentils (urad lentils)
½ cup chopped tofu
½ teaspoon chili powder (according to taste)
2 teaspoons salt (according to taste)
½ teaspoon turmeric powder
1 onion, chopped (optional)
1 large tomato, chopped
1 tablespoon chopped green pepper
2 tablespoons chopped coriander leaves
1 tablespoon chopped ginger
1 teaspoon mango powder (amchur), or 3 tablespoons lemon juice
½ teaspooon garam masala
about 5 to 6 cups water

For the seasoning (tarka)

3 tablespoons soy oil
½ teaspoon cumin seeds
½ teaspoon mustard seeds
2 whole red peppers
2 big cardamoms broken in 2 pieces
1 bay leaf
pinch of asafetida

1. Wash black gram lentils, add salt, turmeric powder, and 5 cups of water and cook for 30 to 40 minutes on slow heat, or until tender.

2. In a pan heat soy oil, add all the seasoning, and fry for a few seconds. Add mashed tofu and ginger and fry until tofu becomes a little brown.

3. Add onion and fry until brown. Then add tomatoes and all the spices except coriander leaves, garam masala, and amchur or lemon. Fry until oil starts oozing out. If needed, add 1 cup water.

4. Mix fried ingredients into the boiled lentils. Mix in garam masala and amchur or lemon juice. Garnish with coriander leaves. Serve warm with bread.

Servings: 6   Time: 40 min.

Nutritional analysis per serving:

Calories	235	(RDA% 12)	Carbohydrate	26 gm
Protein	11 gm	(RDA% 25)	Fat	10 gm

Soy Curry

With Vegetables
Soybean Sambhar

Soybean sambhar is a South Indian delicacy that is a combination of vegetables in a soy curry. Sambhar is enjoyed with dosa and idli.

½ cup soybeans
1½ cups toovar lentils
½ teaspoon baking soda (optional)
about 12 to 14 cups water

Spices

1 teaspoon chili powder (according to taste)
4 teaspoons salt (according to taste)
½ teaspoon turmeric powder
2 tablespoons coconut powder
½ cup lemon juice (according to taste)
2 teaspoons sambhar powder (optional)
1 tablespoon chopped ginger
4 tablespoons chopped coriander leaves

Vegetables

1 cup green beans, diced
½ cup cut carrots, diced
1 cup chopped zucchini (louki)
¼ cup sweet green pepper cut into small pieces

For seasoning (tarka)

2 chopped onions (optional)
2 chopped tomatoes
3 tablespoons soy oil
1 teaspoon mustard seeds
½ teaspoon cumin seeds
pinch of asafetida

1. Soak soybeans for 5 to 6 hours (or cook for 10 to 20 minutes in a pressure cooker). Wash toovar lentils and soybeans. Add 4 to 5 cups of water and baking soda, then bring to a boil over high heat. Reduce the heat to low and cook for 1 hour (use pressure cooker for quick cooking).

3. In a heavy pan place all the vegetables and 3 cups of water. Cook until tender.

4. Heat soy oil in a large pan. Add cumin seeds, mustard seeds, and asafetida and fry for a few seconds. Add onion and fry

until golden brown. Add tomatoes and all the spices, except coriander leaves, and cook 5 to 6 minutes.

5. Mix boiled vegetables with boiled soy lentils and toovar lentils. Cook for 10 to 15 minutes, stirring constantly. Add cooked tomato paste (from No. 4 above) and mix thoroughly.

6. Garnish with coriander leaves and serve warm with dosa or idli.

Servings: 10   Time: 60 min.

Nutritional analysis per serving:

Calories	225	(RDA% 11)
Protein	14 gm	(RDA% 32)
Carbohydrate	27 gm	
Fat	7 gm	

Soy Drinks

THE WONDERS OF soybeans never cease to be amazing; a legume can be used to make one of the most traditional foods, milk and yogurt.

For a few individuals the substitution of soy milk for cow's milk is life sustaining, since they are allergic to cow's milk. Also as individuals become older, they develop intolerance to lactose, which is the sugar found in cow's milk. This intolerance causes indigestion, flatulence, and even diarrhea. Some 90 percent of the adult Oriental population, 80 percent of the Indian population and 40 percent of the Caucasian population have lactose intolerance. For these people soy milk is an excellent substitute.

Though at first try pure soy milk will not suit your palate, it is the only milk used in China. In the recipes we suggest you start with 50 percent soy milk and 50 percent cow's milk. With this the change in taste, texture and color is hardly noticeable.

Only a few of the favorite Indian milk and yogurt recipes are presented here. Soy milk can be combined with saffron, cardamom or rose essence to accompany a bed-time snack. Fruit drinks such as pineapple, mango and banana shakes are easy to make and delightful for kids. Thandai, a spicy soy drink, is a favorite for festivals and holidays.

There are several soy yogurt recipes, both sweet and spicy. Both sweet lassi and salty lassi are musts for the curious palate.

Soy Milk

With Rose Essence

An elegant way to serve soy milk is with rose essence.

4 cups soy milk
4 tablespoons sugar (according to taste)
4 drops of rose essence

Mix ingredients together. Serve with crushed ice.

Servings: 4   Time: 15 min.

Nutritional analysis per serving:

Calories	171	(RDA% 9)
Protein	10 gm	(RDA% 23)
Carbohydrate	21 gm	
Fat	6 gm	

Banana Shake

At our summer lawn party we enjoy soy shakes with banana, mango and pineapple. They make refreshing light drinks.

2 cups soy milk
1 cup cold water
½ cup sugar (according to taste)
1 ripe banana, cut up

1. Combine all the ingredients in a blender jar and blend until smooth.

2. Pour the shake into glasses. Serve with crushed ice.

Servings: 4   Time: 15 min.

Nutritional analysis per serving:

Calories	225	(RDA% 11)
Protein	5 gm	(RDA% 12)
Carbohydrate	47 gm	
Fat	3 gm	

Soy Milk Drink

2 cups soy milk
2 tablespoons sugar (according to taste)
¼ teaspoon fennel seeds
½ inch stick of cinnamon

1. Boil milk, fennel seeds and cinnamon together for 10 minutes, and stir.
2. Strain the milk and add sugar. Serve it hot or cold.

Servings: 2   Time: 15 min.

Nutritional analysis per serving:

Calories	171	(RDA% 9)
Protein	10 gm	(RDA% 23)
Carbohydrate	20 gm	
Fat	5 gm	

Soy Milk
With Saffron and Nuts
Kesar Pista Soy Doodh

4 cups soy milk
½ teaspoon cardamom powder
5 tablespoons sugar (according to taste)
2 tablespoons pistachios and almonds cut into slivers
2 pinches of saffron

1. Combine milk, cardamom powder, saffron and sugar in a heavy pot and bring to a boil. Turn heat low and simmer the milk for 2 minutes.
2. Mix at high speed to make froth. Pour into four glasses. Sprinkle the nuts over the froth and serve immediately.

Servings: 4   Time: 15 min.

Nutritional analysis per serving:

Calories	206	(RDA% 10)
Protein	11 gm	(RDA% 25)
Carbohydrate	25 gm	
Fat	8 gm	

Mango Shake

Mango is one of the most popular fruits in India. During the summer every housewife makes mango shakes at least once a day.

1 cup soy milk
1 cup mango pulp
2 cups water
¼ cup sugar (according to taste)
2 teaspoons pistachios
1 teaspoon cardamom powder
pinch of saffron

1. Combine all the ingredients except pistachios in a blender jar and blend until smooth.
2. Pour into glasses, over crushed ice. Sprinkle the pistachios over the shake and serve.

Servings: 4   Time: 15 min.

Nutritional analysis per serving:

Calories	133	(RDA% 7)
Protein	4 gm	(RDA% 8)
Carbohydrate	24 gm	
Fat	4 gm	

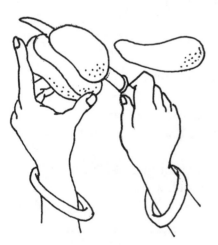

A Slice mango to form pulp.

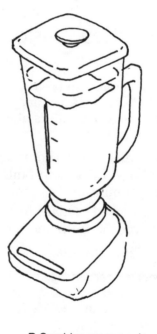

B Combine mango pulp, soy milk, water and sugar. Blend until smooth.

Spicy Soy Drink
Thandai

In India at the spring festival of colors thandai, which is a spicy soy drink, is made in most households.

1½ cups soy milk
½ cup plain milk
3 cups water
7 tablespoons sugar (according to taste)

For paste

2 tablespoons fennel seeds
2 teaspoons black pepper (according to your taste)
4 cardamoms
1 cup water

1. Soak all the ingredients for the paste for 2 to 3 hours. Blend into a fine paste.
2. Mix the paste, milk, sugar, and 2 cups of water. Strain the mixture and serve with crushed ice.

Servings: 3   Time: 20 min.

Nutritional analysis per serving:

Calories	193	(RDA% 10)
Protein	6 gm	(RDA% 14)
Carbohydrate	34 gm	
Fat	4 gm	

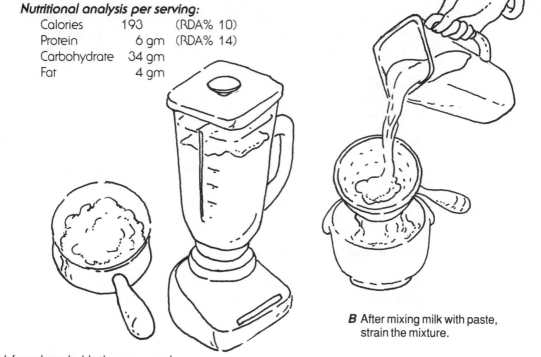

B After mixing milk with paste, strain the mixture.

A Soak fennel seeds, black pepper, and cardamoms in water. Blend into a paste.

Pineapple Shake

2 cups soy milk
1 cup cold water
½ cup sugar (according to taste)
1 cup pineapple, cut into cubes
½ cup fresh coconut

1. Combine all the ingredients in a blender jar and blend until everything is smooth.
2. Pour the shake into glasses. Serve with crushed ice.

Servings: 4   Time: 10 min.

Nutritional analysis per serving:

Calories	231	(RDA% 12)
Protein	6 gm	(RDA% 5)
Carbohydrate	39 gm	
Fat	7 gm	

Sweet Soy-Yogurt Drink
Sweet Lassi

Yogurt and soy milk combine to make lassi, one of India's most savored drinks. This combination can be made into a sweet lassi drink, with cardamom and saffron, or into salty lassi by adding salt and cumin seeds.

1 cup plain yogurt
1 cup soy yogurt
¼ cup sugar (according to taste)
½ teaspoon cardamom powder
pinch of saffron (optional)

1. Combine all ingredients in a blender jar and blend for one minute.
2. Pour into glasses and serve with crushed ice.

Servings: 2   Time: 10 min.

Nutritional analysis per serving:

Calories	219	(RDA% 11)
Protein	9 gm	(RDA% 20)
Carbohydrate	34 gm	
Fat	7 gm	

Thick Salty Soy-Yogurt Drink

Thick Salty Lassi

1 cup soy yogurt
1 cup plain yogurt
½ cup cold water
1 teaspoon salt (according to taste)
1 teaspoon roasted and ground cumin seeds

1. Combine all ingredients in a blender jar and blend for one minute.
2. Pour into glasses and serve with crushed ice.

Servings: 3   Time: 15 min.

Nutritional analysis per serving:

Calories	86	(RDA% 4)
Protein	6 gm	(RDA% 14)
Carbohydrate	6 gm	
Fat	4 gm	

Salty Soy-Yogurt Drink

Salty Lassi

1 cup soy yogurt
1 cup plain yogurt
1 cup water
1 teaspoon salt
1 teaspoon roasted and ground cumin seeds

1. Combine all the ingredients, except cumin seeds, in the blender jar and blend for 1 minute. You can mix it with a wire whisk also.
2. Pour into glasses and sprinkle with roasted cumin seeds. Serve with crushed ice.

Servings: 3   Time: 15 min.

Nutritional analysis per serving:

Calories	86	(RDA% 4)
Protein	6 gm	(RDA% 14)
Carbohydrate	6 gm	
Fat	4 gm	

Soy Desserts

DESSERTS ARE THE MOST irresistible part of the meal and the Indian cuisine has the finest desserts in the world. From a health watcher's viewpoint desserts may not be the most nutritious food, however a simple rule is to enjoy desserts in moderation rather than be tempted from abstinence.

Several general preparations are burfi (cheese diamonds), halva (pudding) and gunja with tofu filling (sweet stuffed tofu pastry). All are mouth-watering desserts which will impress your guests.

Burfi, tofu cheese diamonds, are easy to prepare and are wonderful in taste and texture. Other burfis such as tofu coconut burfi and chocolate tofu burfi are made in a similar manner. By no means let the recipes in this book limit you; experiment with the wide possibilities to suit your personal taste.

Soy foods provide several nutritious ingredients to make an extraordinary variety of puddings. Soy milk puddings include vermicelli pudding with soy milk, rice pudding with soy milk (kheer) and cracked wheat pudding with soy milk (dalia). Yogurt pudding, or soy yogurt shrikhand, is equally delightful, as is pudding made from soy okra.

Halva is a dessert for special occasions. Soybean halva has a rich flavor which even a discriminating mother-in-law can't tell apart from the famed almond halva. Carrot and squash with tofu can be used to make halva, creating a wonderful mix of sweets and vegetables.

171

Tofu Cheese Diamonds
Tofu Burfi

Tofu cheese diamonds are traditional Indian sweets and are easy to prepare.

2 cups tofu
4 cups milk
1 cup sugar (according to taste)
2 tablespoons chopped almonds and pistachios
¼ teaspoon cardamom powder

1. Blend milk and tofu to a smooth paste. In a heavy pan cook the paste over medium heat for 20 to 30 minutes, or until mixture becomes thick. Stir intermittently to prevent sticking.

2. Add sugar and cardamom to the thick paste. Cook and stir constantly for 10 minutes or until all the liquid has evaporated. Remove from heat and spread the mixture in a ½-inch thick layer on a greased plate. Decorate with almonds and pistachios.

3. After half an hour cut into small diamond shapes. Serve cold.

Servings: 8   Time: 50 min.

Nutritional analysis per serving:

Calories	209	(RDA% 10)
Protein	8 gm	(RDA% 18)
Carbohydrate	31 gm	
Fat	7 gm	

Tofu Coconut Diamonds

Tofu Khopra Burfi

After the services at the temple, the priest gives the worshipers some "prasad," which is a blessed offering from the Gods. This offering usually includes coconut burfi.

1½ cups grated coconut (sweetened, unsweetened, or fresh)
2 cups mashed tofu
3 cups plain milk
¼ teaspoon cardamom powder
1¼ cups sugar (according to taste; if coconut is sweetened, use only
    1 cup sugar)

1. Blend milk and tofu to a smooth paste. Soak coconut for 1 hour in the paste.
2. In a heavy pan cook soaked coconut mixture on medium heat about 30 to 40 minutes, or until the mixture becomes thick. Stir intermittently to prevent sticking.
3. Add sugar and cardamom to the thick paste. Cook and stir constantly for 10 to 15 minutes until all the liquid has evaporated. Remove from heat and spread the mixture in a ½-inch thick layer on a greased plate.
4. Allow it to cool and cut into diamond shapes. Serve cold.

Servings: 8   Time: 40 min.

Nutritional analysis per serving:

Calories	289	(RDA% 14)
Protein	7 gm	(RDA% 16)
Carbohydrate	44 gm	
Fat	11 gm	

Tofu Chocolate Diamonds

Tofu Chocolate Burfi

Chocolate tofu burfi is a modern version of a traditional dish. It is especially popular with chocolate lovers.

2 cups ricotta cheese
2 cups tofu
1 cup milk
1 cup sugar
2 tablespoons chocolate powder or cocoa powder, unsweetened

1. Blend all the ingredients (except chocolate powder and sugar) into a smooth paste.
2. In a heavy pan cook the paste over medium heat for 20 to 30 minutes or until paste becomes thick. Stir constantly to prevent sticking.
3. Add sugar to the thick paste. Cook and stir constantly for 10 minutes or until all the liquid has evaporated.
4. Spread half of the batter on a greased plate. Mix chocolate powder in the other half of the batter and spread on top of the white burfi.
5. Allow it to cool. Cut burfi into diamond shapes. Serve cold.

Servings: 8   Time: 50 min.

Nutritional analysis per serving:

Calories	244	(RDA% 12)
Protein	12 gm	(RDA% 27)
Carbohydrate	31 gm	
Fat	10 gm	

Rice Pudding
With Soy Milk
Kheer

Rice pudding with soy milk is elegantly decorated with chopped almonds and pistachios with the aroma of cardamom. Best enjoyed on "sarad purnima," a full-moon night.

3 cups soy milk
3 cups plain milk
1 cup sugar (according to taste)
⅓ cup rice
4 tablespoons chopped almonds and pistachios
½ teaspoon cardamom powder
pinch of saffron

1. In a heavy pan boil the soy milk and plain milk. Wash rice and add to the milk. Stir over medium heat for 30 to 40 minutes until the rice is cooked. If mixture becomes very thick, add ½ cup water or milk.
2. Add sugar and mix well. Dissolve the saffron in one tablespoon water or milk and mix into the kheer.
3. Decorate with chopped almonds and pistachios. Serve warm or chilled.

Servings: 8   Time: 50 min.

Nutritional analysis per serving:

Calories	217	(RDA% 11)
Protein	8 gm	(RDA% 17)
Carbohydrate	32 gm	
Fat	7 gm	

Vermicelli Pudding
With Soy Milk
Sevaiyan Kheer

Vermicelli pudding is a special treat on Iid, the holiest day for the Moslems.

3 cups soy milk
3 cups plain milk
½ cup vermicelli, broken into 1-inch pieces
1 tablespoon vegetable shortening
1¼ cups sugar (according to taste)
3 teaspoons chopped pistachios and almonds
¼ teaspoon cardamom powder
pinch of saffron

1. In a small pan heat vegetable shortening. Add vermicelli and roast over low heat until light brown.
2. In a heavy pan boil the soy milk and plain milk, then add vermicelli. Stir over medium heat for 20 minutes, until the mixture is thick, then remove from heat.
3. Dissolve the saffron in 1 teaspoon water or milk and add to the cooked sevaiyan kheer. Decorate with chopped almonds and pistachios. Serve warm or chilled.

Servings: 6   Time: 50 min.

Nutritional analysis per serving:

Calories	342	(RDA% 17)
Protein	10 gm	(RDA% 23)
Carbohydrate	58 gm	
Fat	9 gm	

Pineapple Pudding
Pineapple Sandesh

My son was amazed to see how quickly and easily he could prepare pineapple sandesh. It is a sure hit even when prepared by an inexperienced cook.

1 cup tofu
1 cup ricotta cheese
1 cup sugar (according to taste)
1 cup pineapple cubes
½ teaspoon cardamom powder
2 tablespoons shredded almonds and pistachio
pinch of saffron

1. Soak the saffron in 2 teaspoons milk. Beat tofu, ricotta cheese, sugar and saffron into a smooth paste.
2. Add pineapple cubes. Decorate with chopped almonds, pistachios and cardamom. Cool in refrigerator for 2 hours before serving.

Servings: 6   Time: 15 min.

Nutritional analysis per serving:

Calories	225	(RDA% 11)
Protein	8 gm	(RDA% 12)
Carbohydrate	39 gm	
Fat	6 gm	

Soy-Yogurt Pudding
Shrikhand

A dish which appears difficult to make, but really takes only minutes to put together. It is a light dish enjoyed in the summer.

4 cups plain yogurt
4 cups soy yogurt
2 cups sugar (according to taste)
½ teaspoon cardamom powder
¼ teaspoon saffron
4 teaspoons chopped almonds and pistachios

1. In cheesecloth put plain yogurt and soy yogurt together. Tie and hang the cheesecloth. Allow the yogurt to drain for 5 to 6 hours.

2. Soak the saffron in 1 tablespoon milk. When all the water drains from cheesecloth, transfer the yogurt to a deep bowl and mix in sugar and saffron with a mixer or heavy spoon.

3. Decorate with pistachios, almonds and cardamom. Cool in refrigerator for 2 hours before serving.

Servings: 8   Time: 20 min.

Nutritional analysis per serving:

Calories	316	(RDA% 16)
Protein	9 gm	(RDA% 21)
Carbohydrate	58 gm	
Fat	7 gm	

Cracked Wheat Pudding

With Soy Milk

Dalia with Soy Milk

A high-fiber dish that tastes good and is enjoyed by the entire family.

½ cup cracked wheat (dalia)
2 cups soy milk
1 cup sugar
¼ teaspoon cardamon powder
2 tablespoons chopped almonds and pistachios
pinch of saffron
about 4 to 5 cups water

1. In a heavy pan boil 4 to 5 cups of water and add cracked wheat. Cover and cook on low heat for 40 to 50 minutes or until dalia is cooked.
2. Add soy milk, sugar and saffron and cook again for 15 to 20 minutes over low heat. Stir to prevent sticking.
3. Decorate with almonds, pistachios and cardamom powder and serve warm.

Servings: 4   Time: 60 min.

Nutritional analysis per serving:

Calories	280	(RDA% 14)
Protein	6 gm	(RDA% 14)
Carbohydrate	56 gm	
Fat	5 gm	

Cracked Wheat Pudding

With Soy Okra

Dalia with Soy Okra

½ cup cracked wheat (dalia)
4½ cups water (approximately)
1 cup soy okra
1 cup brown sugar
¼ teaspoon cardamom powder

1. Prepare this pudding in the same manner as Sweet Pudding with Soy Milk, substituting soy okra for soy milk.
2. When pudding is prepared, add sugar and cardamom powder, and cook for another 5 minutes. Serve warm.

Servings: 4   Time: 60 min.

Nutritional analysis per serving:

Calories	257	(RDA% 13)
Protein	3 gm	(RDA% 6)
Carbohydrate	62 gm	
Fat	1 gm	

Tofu Sweet Pudding
Tofu Kalakand

Another one of India's most savored sweet dishes.

1 cup tofu
2 cups mik
¾ cup sugar (according to taste)
¼ teaspoon cardamom powder
2 tablespoons chopped almonds and pistachios
pinch of saffron
¼ cup water

1. Blend milk and tofu into a smooth paste.
2. In a heavy pan cook paste over medium heat for 20 to 30 minutes, until mixture becomes thick. Stir intermittently to prevent sticking. Allow to cool.
3. In another pan add sugar, saffron, and ¼ cup water and cook until sugar dissolves to make syrup. Allow syrup to cool and add to paste.
4. Place kalakand in a serving dish and garnish with almonds, pistachios and cardamom. Chill before serving.

Servings: 6   Time: 50 min.

Nutritional analysis per serving:

Calories	177	(RDA% 9)
Protein	6 gm	(RDA% 13)
Carbohydrate	29 gm	
Fat	5 gm	

Soybean Pudding
Soybean Halva

Ready-made halva can be found in health-food stores, but it cannot be compared to the traditional halva, which has a rich and distinctive flavor. Even the most particular mother-in-law cannot question the taste of this soybean halva.

¼ cup mung lentils
1 cup dry soybeans
4 teaspoons chopped almonds and pistachios
¼ teaspoon cardamom powder
2 cups sugar
1¼ cups butter
3 cups water
pinch of saffron

1. Wash and soak soybeans and mung dal in warm water overnight or for 6 to 8 hours. Drain and wash again. Blend into a paste. Add a little water if needed.
2. In a heavy frying pan heat butter. Add paste and stir constantly about 30 to 40 minutes, or until golden brown.
3. Add 3 cups of water, cook for 4 to 6 minutes. Add sugar and saffron and cook again. Stir over low heat until most of the liquid has evaporated and butter rises to the surface. Remove from heat, and garnish with almonds and cardamom. Serve warm.

Servings: 10   Time: 120 min.

Nutritional analysis per serving:

Calories	396	(RDA% 20)
Protein	12 gm	(RDA% 26)
Carbohydrate	47 gm	
Fat	20 gm	

Carrot Halva

Gajar Ka Halva

Carrot halva is our favorite recipe at soy cooking demonstrations. It has impressed many people with its sweet taste and appealing color.

4 cups grated carrots
1½ cups mashed tofu
3 cups milk
1½ cups sugar (according to taste)
2 tablespoons chopped almonds and pistachios
½ teaspoon ground cardamom
3 tablespoons butter
pinch of saffron

1. Blend milk and tofu into a smooth paste.
2. In a heavy saucepan, heat butter. Add carrots and paste. Cook over medium heat, and stir intermittently for 30 to 40 minutes until the mixture becomes thick.
3. Add sugar, saffron and cardamom to the thick paste. Cook and stir constantly for 10 minutes until all the liquid has evaporated.
4. Place in a dish and decorate with almonds and pistachios. Serve cold or warm.

Servings: 8   Time: 50 min.

Nutritional analysis per serving:

Calories	454	(RDA% 23)
Protein	7 gm	(RDA% 16)
Carbohydrate	47 gm	
Fat	29 gm	

A Grate carrots.

B Cook carrot and paste over medium heat. Stir intermittently.

Pastry
Stuffed with Tofu
Gunja

In India, a week before Diwali, the festival of light, my mother would make gunjas and store them safely away from the children. Then, on Diwali day, when friends and relatives arrived, we would exchange and enjoy the sweets.

For dough

2 cups all-purpose flour
4 tablespoons vegetable shortening
approximately ½ cup water
vegetable shortening for deep-frying

For filling

1 cup tofu
2 cups milk
1 cup sugar (according to taste)
1 cup coconut (unsweetened)
¼ cup raisins
2 tablespoons chopped almonds
½ teaspoon cardamom powder

1. Blend milk and tofu into a smooth paste. Cook over medium heat for 20 to 25 minutes until the mixture is thick. Stir intermittently to prevent sticking. Allow paste to cool, then add the other ingredients for the filling.

2. Combine all-purpose flour and 4 tablespoons of vegetable shortening in a bowl and mix well. Add a little water at a time to make a stiff dough. Knead dough for 3 to 4 minutes. Cover and set aside for 15 minutes.

3. Knead the dough for 2 minutes and make 18 to 20 equal-size balls. Roll each ball in a very thin circle of 3 to 4 inches in diameter.

4. Place about 1½ tablespoons of the filling mixture on half of a circle. Wet the edge of the other half of the circle and fold it over to make a stuffed semicircle. Press the seam with fingers and then gently press with a fork. Make all the gunjas and cover them with plastic wrap until ready to fry.

5. In a heavy frying pan heat vegetable shortening over medium heat. Fry gunjas over low heat, until they are golden brown on

both sides. Take them out and drain on paper towels. Cool, and store in an airtight container or cookie jar. Serve cold.

Servings: 10   Time: 90 min.

Nutritional analysis per serving:

Calories	362	(RDA% 18)
Protein	6 gm	(RDA% 14)
Carbohydrate	47 gm	
Fat	18 gm	

Zucchini Halva

Louki Ka Halva

4 cups grated zucchini
1½ cups mashed tofu
3 cups milk
1½ cups sugar
2 tablespoons slivered almonds and pistachios
½ teaspoon ground cardamom
3 tablespoons butter
pinch of saffron

1. Blend milk and tofu into a smooth paste.
2. In a heavy saucepan, heat butter. Add grated zucchini and the tofu paste. Cook over medium heat and stir intermittently for 30 to 40 minutes until the mixture becomes thick.
3. Add sugar, saffron and cardamom to the thick paste. Cook and stir constantly for 10 minutes until all the liquid has evaporated.
4. Place in a dish and decorate with almonds and pistachios. Serve cold or warm.

Servings: 8   Time: 50 min.

Nutritional analysis per serving:

Calories	275	(RDA% 14)
Protein	7 gm	(RDA% 16)
Carbohydrate	43 gm	
Fat	10 gm	

Tofu Pancakes in Syrup
Malpua with Tofu

1 cup soy milk
¾ cup all-purpose flour (maida)
¾ cup sugar
3 tablespoons mixed nuts for decoration
½ teaspoon cardamom powder
½ cup water
vegetable shortening for frying

1. Mix all-purpose flour and soy milk and stir for 3 minutes. Keep in a warm place for 2 hours.
2. In a heavy pan cook sugar with ½ cup water for 15 to 20 minutes, or until the sugar dissolves.
3. In a frying pan heat the vegetable shortening. Drop one big spoonful of mixture in the pan and flatten it. Fry both sides until light brown. Make all pancakes in a similar manner.
4. Dip pancakes into the syrup for 2 minutes. Arrange on serving plate. Decorate with nuts and serve warm.

Servings: 6   Time: 60 min.

Nutritional analysis per serving:

Calories	340	(RDA% 17)
Protein	4 gm	(RDA% 8)
Carbohydrate	58 gm	
Fat	12 gm	

Mango Pudding
Mango Kalakand

Mango, the favorite summer fruit of the East, can be incorporated into a delicious sweet pudding loved by children of all ages.

2 medium-size ripe mangoes
1 cup tofu, mashed
1 cup sugar
¼ teaspoon cardamom powder
pinch of saffron

1. Peel and grate the mangoes. Remove all the pulp from the pit.

2. In a heavy pan put mango pulp and tofu and cook over medium heat for 45 minutes, until paste becomes thick. Stir intermittently to prevent sticking.

3. Add sugar and saffron to the thick paste. Cook and stir constantly for 5 to 8 minutes. Place in a serving dish, garnish with cardamom and serve cold.

Servings: 4   Time: 50 min.

Nutritional analysis per serving:

Calories	280	(RDA% 14)
Protein	4 gm	(RDA% 9)
Carbohydrate	67 gm	
Fat	2 gm	

Soy Sweet Pearls >

Soy Sweet Pearls
Soy Flour Bundi

Soy flour bundies are sweet, brightly colored pearls that will add a decorative touch to any table.

1½ cups chick-pea flour
¾ cup soy flour
1¼ cups water
soy oil for deep-frying

For syrup

3 cups sugar
2 cups water
yellow food coloring

For decoration

½ teaspoon cardamom powder
1 tablespoon slivered almonds

1. In a heavy pan add sugar, water and a few drops of yellow food coloring. Cook for 15 to 20 minutes, or until the sugar dissolves.
2. Combine chick-pea flour, soy flour and water in a bowl. Beat for 3 to 5 minutes until batter becomes light and smooth.
3. Heat soy oil in a deep frying pan. Hold strainer or colander about 4 inches above the oil. Pour ½ cup batter at a time into the strainer. Batter will fall in the form of very fine drops into the hot oil. Fry for one minute or until bundi becomes a little brown.
4. Take bundies out and put in warm syrup for 6 to 8 minutes, or until they absorb the syrup and swell slightly. Remove from syrup and arrange on a plate.
5. Decorate with cardamom powder and almonds, and serve warm or cold.

Servings: 15   Time: 40 min.

Nutritional analysis per serving:

Calories	273	(RDA% 17)
Protein	4 gm	(RDA% 10)
Carbohydrate	47 gm	
Fat	5 gm	

Soy Flour Sweet Diamonds

Sweet Shakerpara

2 cups all-purpose flour
½ cup soy flour
⅓ cup oil
about ½ cup water
oil for deep-frying

For syrup

1½ cup sugar
½ cup water

1. Combine soy flour, all-purpose flour and oil and mix well. Add enough water to make a stiff dough.
2. Divide the dough in two parts and roll them into ⅙-inch thick sheets. Cut the rolled dough first straight and then diagonally, so as to get small diamond-shaped pieces.
3. In a heavy saucepan heat the soy oil. Fry diamonds on slow heat until they turn brown. Place them on a towel.
4. In heavy saucepan boil sugar and ½ cup water. Boil on low heat for 15 to 20 minutes until it becomes a thick syrup.
5. Put half of the fried diamonds in the syrup pan and cover with syrup. After 10 minutes take the coated diamonds out and place the remaining diamonds in the syrup.
6. Place diamonds separately on a plate to dry. When dried put them in a covered container. Serve any time as a sweet snack.

Servings: 8   Time: 40 min.

Nutritional analysis per serving:

Calories	390	(RDA% 20)
Protein	5 gm	(RDA% 12)
Carbohydrate	60 gm	
Fat	16 gm	

Sweet Soy Flour Balls
Laddu

Laddu is the favorite sweet for religious holidays in India.

1 cup soy flour
1 cup chick-pea flour
¾ cup butter
1¼ cups sugar (according to taste)
½ teaspoon cardamom powder
2 tablespoons almonds

1. In a heavy pan melt butter on slow heat and add soy flour and chick-pea flour. Stir the flour until it becomes light brown in color or appears roasted. Then allow to cool.
2. Once flour is cool, add sugar, cardamom and almonds and mix. Take ⅓ cup mixture in palm, press with both hands and roll into a tight ball. Store the balls in an air-tight container. Serve as a sweet snack.

Servings: 10   Time: 50 min.

Nutritional analysis per serving:

Calories	278	(RDA% 14)
Protein	6 gm	(RDA% 14)
Carbohydrate	33 gm	
Fat	15 gm	

Soy Ice Cream, Cookies and Cakes

ICE CREAM, cookies and cakes are Western dishes exported to the East, where they have been incorporated with indigenous recipes.

A unique feature of these recipes is the addition of soy flour, tofu and soy milk. The latter is an essential element for the lactose-intolerant individual who cannot enjoy ice cream made from cow's milk. Soy is also important for the low cholesterol diet. Soy products, being 100 percent cholesterol-free, provide an added advantage when partaking of the pleasures of cakes, cookies and ice cream.

Tofu Ice Cream

1½ cups tofu
1 cup milk
¾ cup sugar
2 tablespoons chopped almonds and pistachios
½ teaspoon cardamom powder
pinch of saffron
4 drops khaskhas (or vanilla) essence

1. Soak the saffron in 1 tablespoon warm milk and blend. Mix milk, sugar, saffron and tofu and blend until smooth. Add khaskhas essence and mix well.
2. Pour the mixture into ice trays. Put in the freezer for an hour, then take it out of the trays and blend again for one minute.
3. Pour it again into ice trays. Decorate with almonds, pistachios and cardamom powder and freeze until firm.

Servings: 6   Time: 30 min.

Nutritional analysis per serving:

Calories	140	(RDA% 7)
Protein	5 gm	(RDA% 11)
Carbohydrate	24 gm	
Fat	4 gm	

Mango Ice Cream

1 cup tofu
1 cup milk
1 cup mango pulp
1½ cups sugar
½ teaspoon cardamom powder
2 tablespoons chopped almonds and pistachios
pinch of saffron

1. Soak the saffron in 1 tablespoon warm milk and crush with a spoon. Mix milk, mango pulp, sugar, saffron and tofu and blend until mixture becomes smooth.
2. Pour the mixture into ice trays. Put in the freezer for an hour; then take it out of the trays and blend again for one minute.
3. Pour it again into ice trays. Decorate with almonds, pistachios and cardamom powder and freeze until firm.

Servings: 6   Time: 20 min.

Nutritional analysis per serving:

Calories	265	(RDA% 13)
Protein	4 gm	(RDA% 10)
Carbohydrate	57 gm	
Fat	4 gm	

Saffron Ice Cream

1 cup tofu
1 cup milk
¾ cup sugar
¼ teaspoon cardamom powder
2 tablespoons chopped almonds and pistachios
big pinch of saffron

Make the saffron ice cream in the same manner as tofu ice cream.

Servings: 6   Time: 30 min.

Nutritional analysis per serving:

Calories	153	(RDA%	8)
Protein	4 gm	(RDA%	10)
Carbohydrate	27 gm		
Fat	4 gm		

Chocolate Ice Cream

2 ounces (2 squares) unsweetened chocolate
1 cup sugar
1½ cups tofu
1 cup milk, heated
2 teaspoons vanilla extract
1 cup heavy cream

1. Heat the chocolate in the top of a double boiler, stirring frequently until it has melted. Add sugar and continue stirring.
2. Blend milk and tofu to a smooth paste. Mix everything together until completely blended. Cool and add vanilla extract. Refrigerate for 1 hour or longer, then pour into an ice tray.
3. Put the ice tray in the freezer for an hour. Then take the mixture out of the tray and blend again for one minute. Pour the mixture again into the ice tray and freeze until firm.

Note: If using ice cream machine, pour mixture into the machine and freeze according to manufacturer's directions.

Servings: 6   Time: 20 min.

Nutritional analysis per serving:

Calories	251	(RDA%	13)
Protein	7 gm	(RDA%	15)
Carbohydrate	9 gm		
Fat	23 gm		

Strawberry Ice Cream

1 cup tofu
1 cup milk
½ cup heavy cream
2 cups fresh strawberries
1½ cups sugar (approximately)

1. Cut up ½ cup of the strawberries. Sprinkle a little sugar over them and keep for decoration. Blend the remaining strawberries, add sugar and mix well. Blend with milk, cream and tofu until mixture becomes smooth.
2. Pour the mixture into ice trays. Put in the freezer for an hour; then take it out of the trays and blend again for one minute.
3. Pour it again into ice trays. Decorate with strawberry slices and freeze until firm.

Servings: 6   Time: 20 min.

Nutritional analysis per serving:

Calories	268	(RDA% 13)
Protein	5 gm	(RDA% 10)
Carbohydrate	55 gm	
Fat	5 gm	

Spicy Soy Cookies

½ cups vegetable shortening
1 cup all-purpose flour
½ cup soy flour
½ cup sugar
1 teaspoon baking soda

½ teaspoon ground cinnamon
¼ teaspoon ground nutmeg
pinch of ground cloves
½ cup raisins
about ½ cup warm milk

1. Beat shortening with sugar for 5 minutes. Add all the other ingredients except milk. Mix well, add warm milk, and form a dough. Make into 1-inch balls, flattened.
2. Grease and flour a cookie sheet and place the cookies 1 to 2 inches apart. Bake for 10 to 12 minutes at 300 F, or until they are done. Remove from baking sheet, cool, and store.

Servings: 10   Time: 20 min.

Nutritional analysis per serving:

Calories	123	(RDA% 6)
Protein	4 gm	(RDA% 9)
Carbohydrate	26 gm	
Fat	1 gm	

Soybean Cookies

2 cups all-purpose flour
1 cup soy flour
1 cup vegetable shortening
1½ cups sugar
1 teaspoon baking soda
1 teaspoon baking powder
½ teaspoon cardamom powder
4 tablespoons chopped pistachios and almonds (optional)
about ¾ cup milk (at room temperature)
pinch of saffron

1. Preheat oven to 300 F Mix baking soda, baking powder, all-purpose flour and soy flour, and set aside.

2. Beat vegetable shortening with sugar for 5 minutes. Add cardamom powder and saffron and mix well. Then add milk and flour mixture and mix well to form dough. Make 45 to 50 1-inch balls, flattened.

3. Grease and flour a cookie sheet and place the cookies about 1 inch apart. Decorate the tops with small pieces of almonds and pistachios and bake for 15 to 18 minutes, or until they are done. Remove from baking sheet, cool, and store.

Servings: 16   Time: 60 min.

Nutritional analysis per serving:

Calories	279	(RDA% 14)
Protein	5 gm	(RDA% 11)
Carbohydrate	32 gm	
Fat	16 gm	

A Sift flour, baking soda and baking powder.

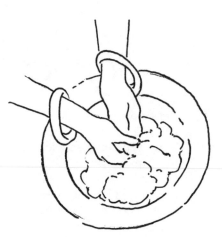

B Combine butter and sugar.

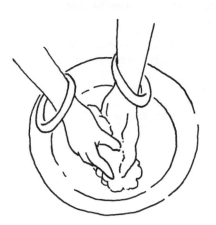

C Beat until it becomes light and creamy.

D From the dough make 18-20 balls.

E Bake on a greased and floured sheet until slightly brown.

Soy Biscuits

Soy Biscuits
Naan Khatai

½ cup all-purpose flour
½ cup soy flour
½ cup butter
¾ cup sugar
½ teaspoon cardamom powder
pinch of baking soda
pinch of baking powder

1. Sift all-purpose flour, soy flour, baking soda and baking powder together.
2. Combine butter and sugar in a bowl and beat until it becomes light and creamy. Mix all the ingredients and knead the dough well.
3. From the dough make 18 to 20 small balls and arrange on a greased and floured baking sheet. Make a cross (x) on the top of each naan khatai with the help of a knife.
4. Bake at 275 F for 10 minutes and then lower the baking temperature to 200 F for 8 minutes, or until naan khatais are slightly brown. Cool and store.

Servings: 10   Time: 20 min.

Nutritional analysis per serving:

Calories	171	(RDA% 9)
Protein	3 gm	(RDA% 6)
Carbohydrate	21 gm	
Fat	9 gm	

Oatmeal Cookies

2 cups all-purpose flour
1 cup soy flour
1 cup oatmeal
1 cup vegetable shortening
1¾ cups sugar
1 teaspoon baking soda
1 teaspoon baking powder
about ¾ cup milk (at room temperature)

1. Preheat oven to 300 F Sift baking soda, baking powder, all-purpose flour and soy flour.
2. Beat vegetable shortening with sugar for 5 minutes. Add flour mixture, milk, and oatmeal and make a dough. Make 50 to 55 1-inch balls flattened.
3. Grease a cookie sheet and put the cookies 1½ inches apart. Bake them for 15 to 20 minutes, or until they are light brown. Take them off the baking sheet, cool, and store.

Servings: 16   Time: 60 min.

Nutritional analysis per serving:

Calories	266	(RDA% 13)
Protein	5 gm	(RDA% 10)
Carbohydrate	36 gm	
Fat	13 gm	

Coconut Cookies

½ cup all-purpose flour
½ cup soy flour
⅓ cup vegetable shortening
½ cup grated coconut
⅓ cup sugar
¾ cups confectioner's sugar
¼ cup chopped pistachios and almonds
½ teaspoon cardamom powder
2 tablespoons hot milk

1. Beat the vegetable shortening and granulated sugar until light and creamy. Add 2 tablespoons of water and beat well.

2. Sift all-purpose flour and soy flour and add to creamed mixture. Add the coconut and knead into a dough.

3. Make 10–15 balls, flatten them, and arrange on a greased cookie sheet. Bake at 350 F for 10 minutes; then lower the baking temperature to 300 F and bake for 5 minutes, or until coconut cookies are light brown. Take them off the baking sheet and cool.

4. Add 2 tablespoons of hot milk to the confectioner's sugar and mix well. Apply this icing on top of each cookie, and spread chopped pistachios, almonds and cardamom powder on the top.

Servings: 10   Time: 60 min.

Nutritional analysis per serving:

Calories	221	(RDA% 11)
Protein	3 gm	(RDA% 7)
Carbohydrate	30 gm	
Fat	11 gm	

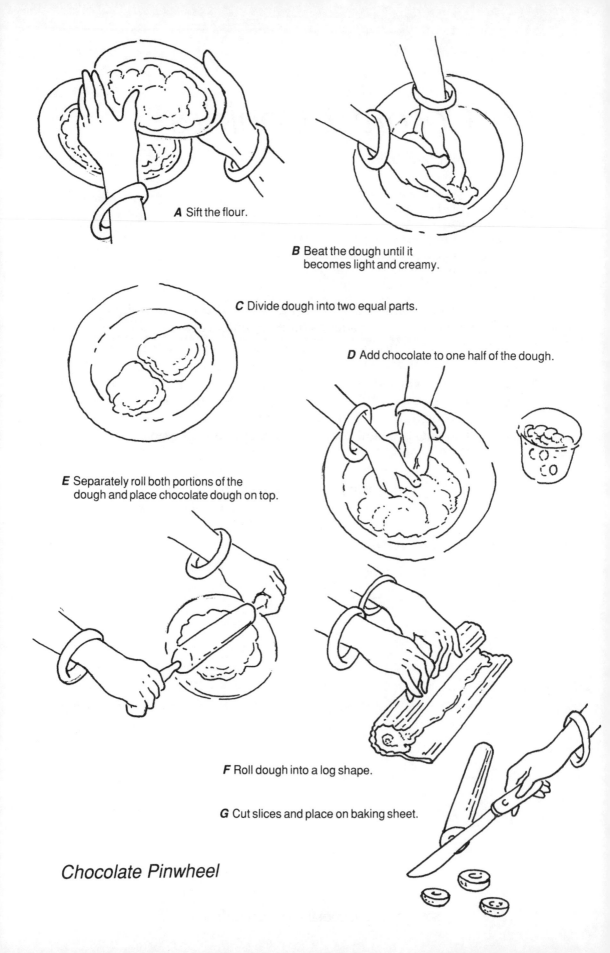

A Sift the flour.

B Beat the dough until it becomes light and creamy.

C Divide dough into two equal parts.

D Add chocolate to one half of the dough.

E Separately roll both portions of the dough and place chocolate dough on top.

F Roll dough into a log shape.

G Cut slices and place on baking sheet.

Chocolate Pinwheel

Chocolate Pinwheels

1 cup all-purpose flour
1 cup soy flour
¾ cup vegetable shortening
1½ cups sugar
1 teaspoon cocoa
2 teaspoons chocolate, grated
2 teaspoons vanilla extract
5 tablespoons water

1. Sift all-purpose flour and soy flour together. Mix the vegetable shortening and sugar in a bowl and beat until light and creamy. Add 5 tablespoons of water and beat again.
2. Add the vanilla extract, soy flour, and all-purpose flour and mix well. Divide the dough into two equal parts. In one part of the dough add chocolate and cocoa.
3. Roll both portions of dough ¼-inch thick. Place the chocolate dough on top. Roll and cut into about ¼-inch thick slices.
4. Arrange the cookies on a greased cookie sheet, and bake at 350 F for 10 minutes. Then lower the baking temperature to 300 F and bake for 15 minutes or until chocolate pinwheels are done.
5. Remove from the baking sheet. Cool and store.

Servings: 16   Time: 60 min.

Nutritional analysis per serving:

Calories	213	(RDA% 11)
Protein	3 gm	(RDA% 8)
Carbohydrate	26 gm	
Fat	12 gm	

Soy and Cream Cheese Cookies

½ cup cream cheese (at room temperature)
1 cup sugar
1½ cups all-purpose flour
1 cup soy flour
1 cup vegetable shortening
2 teaspoons vanilla extract
red or green sugar if desired

1. Beat the vegetable shortening, cream cheese, granulated sugar and vanilla extract until light and fluffy.
2. Add flour and mix together to make dough. Divide dough into 2 equal portions. Wrap and keep in the refrigerator for 2 hours, or until firm.
3. Take the dough out of the refrigerator and allow it to stand at room temperature until soft enough to roll.
4. Preheat oven to 350 F Roll the dough on a floured surface until it is about ¼-inch thick. Cut into desired shapes and place on ungreased baking sheets. Sprinkle with red or green sugar and bake 6 to 8 minutes, or until edges are golden. Remove cookies from sheets and cool on a rack.

Servings: 16   Time: 20 min.

Nutritional analysis per serving:

Calories	256	(RDA% 13)
Protein	5 gm	(RDA% 12)
Carbohydrate	23 gm	
Fat	16 gm	

Carrot Cake

1½ cups all-purpose flour
½ cup tofu
1 cup carrots, grated
¾ cup milk
1 cup sugar
⅓ cup soy oil
½ teaspoon vanilla extract
1 teaspoon baking powder
½ teaspoon baking soda
½ teaspoon cardamom powder
3 tablespoons slivered almonds and pistachios

1. Blend tofu and milk together in blender to make a smooth paste. Sift the flour, baking powder and baking soda together.
2. Mix all the ingredients together, except almonds and pistachios. Beat well for 2 to 3 minutes.
3. Grease and flour an 8-inch-diameter pan and pour the mixture into the pan.
4. Preheat the oven to 350 F, then bake the cake for 15 minutes. Remove from oven and garnish with cut almonds and pistachios. Then reduce the temperature to 300 F and continue baking for another 20 to 25 minutes, or until a wooden pick or knife inserted in center of cake comes out clean.
5. Cool in pan on a wire rack for 2 minutes. Invert pan on a serving plate and leave for 3 to 4 minutes. Carefully remove pan. Invert the cake, cut into slices, and serve.

Servings: 6   Time: 50 min.

Nutritional analysis per serving:

Calories	294	(RDA% 15)
Protein	5 gm	(RDA% 11)
Carbohydrate	44 gm	
Fat	12 gm	

Sponge Cake

1 cup self-rising flour
⅓ cup soy flour
¼ cup vegetable shortening
1 cup condensed milk
1 teaspoon baking powder
½ teaspoon baking soda
½ teaspoon vanilla extract
⅓ cup milk
icing of your choice, if desired

1. Sift the flours, baking powder and soda together. Mix all ingredients except milk, then add ⅓ cup milk and beat well.
2. Grease and flour an 8-inch-diameter pan. Pour the mixture into the pan.
3. Preheat the oven to 350 F, then bake the cake for 12 minutes. Reduce the temperature to 300 F and bake for 10 to 12 minutes, or until a wooden pick or knife inserted in center of cake comes out clean.
4. Place pan on a wire rack and cool for 2 minutes. Invert pan on a serving plate and leave for 3 to 4 minutes. Carefully remove pan, then invert the cake. Add icing, if desired, and serve.

Servings: 6   Time: 50 min.

Nutritional analysis per serving:

Calories	360	(RDA% 18)
Protein	9 gm	(RDA% 19)
Carbohydrate	45 gm	
Fat	17 gm	

Pineapple Upside-Down Cake

6 slices canned pineapple, well drained
6 cherries
1 cup soy flour
1½ cups all-purpose flour
1 cup granulated sugar
2 teaspoons baking powder
½ cup butter or vegetable shortening
1 cup milk
1 teaspoon vanilla extract
sweetened whipped cream, if desired.

1. Sift the soy flour, all-purpose flour and baking powder together. Mix all ingredients, except pineapple slices and cherries, and beat well, about 5 minutes.

2. Grease and flour an 8-inch pan. Arrange pineapple slices in the greased pan. Place one cherry in center of each pineapple slice. Pour batter evenly over pineapple slices.

3. Preheat the oven to 350 F, then bake the cake for 15 minutes. Reduce the temperature to 300 F and bake for 10 to 15 minutes, or until a wooden pick or knife inserted in center of cake comes out clean.

4. Cool in pan on a wire rack for 2 minutes. Invert pan on a serving plate and leave for 3 to 4 minutes. Carefully remove pan. Do not invert cake (pineapple slices should be on top). Cut into slices and serve with sweetened whipped cream, if desired.

Servings: 6   Time: 50 min.

Nutritional analysis per serving:

Calories	276	(RDA% 14)
Protein	7 gm	(RDA% 17)
Carbohydrate	34 gm	
Fat	14 gm	

Chocolate Cake

1½ cups all-purpose flour
½ cup soy flour
1 cup sugar
½ cup vegetable shortening
1 cup milk
½ teaspoon vanilla extract
1 teaspoon baking powder
½ teaspoon baking soda
1 tablespoon cocoa
1 tablespoon grated chocolate

For chocolate glacé icing

1 cup confectioner's sugar
2 teaspoons cocoa
1 tablespoon grated chocolate
1 teaspoon butter
2 tablespoons warm water or milk

For decoration

walnuts, cherries and silver balls

1. Sift the flours, baking soda, baking powder, chocolate and cocoa together. In a bowl, beat sugar and shortening very well. When it is light and creamy, add flour mixture and milk, and beat for 3 to 4 minutes. Add vanilla extract.

2. Grease and flour an 8-inch-diameter pan, and pour the mixture into the pan.

3. Preheat the oven to 350 F, then bake the cake for 15 minutes. Reduce the temperature to 300 F and bake for 10 to 15 minutes, or until a wooden pick or knife inserted in center of cake comes out clean.

4. When cake is cool, mix all icing ingredients together except water or milk. Add water or milk a little at a time and beat for one minute.

5. Ice the cake, decorate with walnuts, cherries and silver balls, and serve.

Servings: 6   Time: 50 min.

Nutritional analysis per serving:

Calories	428	(RDA% 21)
Protein	6 gm	(RDA% 13)
Carbohydrate	68 gm	
Fat	16 gm	

Banana Cake

1½ cups all-purpose flour
½ cup soy flour
1 cup bananas, mashed
½ cup milk
1 cup sugar
½ cup vegetable shortening
½ teaspoon vanilla extract
1 teaspoon baking powder
½ teaspoon baking soda
¼ cup slivered almonds (optional)

1. Sift the flour, soy flour, baking powder and baking soda together. Mix all ingredients together except almonds, and beat well for about 5 minutes.
2. Grease and flour an 8-inch-diameter pan; pour the mixture into the pan.
3. Preheat the oven to 350 F, then bake the cake for 15 minutes. Reduce the temperature to 300 F and bake for 10 to 15 minutes, or until a wooden pick or knife inserted in center of cake comes out clean.
4. Cool in pan on a wire rack for 2 minutes. Invert pan on a serving plate and leave for 3 to 4 minutes. Carefully remove pan, then invert the cake. Cut into slices and serve.

Servings: 8   Time: 60 min.

Nutritional analysis per serving:

Calories	278	(RDA% 14)
Protein	6 gm	(RDA% 14)
Carbohydrate	48 gm	
Fat	8 gm	

Suggested Menus

The following are some of the suggested menus for a traditional meal. The heart of an Indian meal is bread, a curried vegetable, a stuffed vegetable, rice and lentils. Appetizer, salad, raita, chutney and dessert make the meal attractive and complete.

Light Meals

(Each of the following four sets of recipes will make a wonderful light meal.)

Chappati (Whole-wheat soy bread)
Urad dal with Tofu (Black gram lentils with tofu)
Bharwa Aloo (Stuffed potatoes with tofu)
Kakri and Tamatar Salad with Tofu (Cucumber, tomato and tofu salad)
Tamatar Chutney (Tomato chutney)
Pineapple Sandesh (Pineapple pudding)

Aloo Paratha (Bread stuffed with potatoes and tofu)
Katcha Tamatar with Tofu (Green tomatoes with tofu)
Kakri Raita (Cucumber raita with soy yogurt)
Dhania Soybean Chutney (Coriander soybean chutney)

Tofu Khichadi (Tofu with rice and lentils)
Plain Soy Yogurt
Palak Tofu Salad (Spinach and tofu salad)
Dhania Tofu Chutney (Coriander tofu chutney)

Soy Idli (Steamed soybean muffins) or Soy Dosa (Soybean and rice pancakes)
Soybean Sambhar (Soy curry with vegetables)
Mung and Soy Sprout Salad
Khopra Soybean Chutney (Coconut soybean chutney)

Heavy Meal

(Two sets of recipes for two hearty meals.)

Chappati (Whole-wheat soy bread)
Rice with Soy Okra
Soy Dal with Kari (Soy lentils with cucumbers)
Bharwa Aloo (Stuffed potatoes with tofu)
Tamatar Soy Raita (Tomato raita with soy yogurt)
Gobhi Tofu Salad (Cauliflower and tofu salad)
Soybean Chutney
Gajar Ka Halva (Carrot pudding)

Soy Paratha (Fried whole-wheat soy bread)
Tofu Rice
Mung Dal with Palak and Soy Okra (Mung lentils with spinach and soy okra)
Bharwa Kela (Stuffed bananas with tofu)
Aloo Tofu Raita (Potato and tofu raita)
Gajar Tofu Salad (Carrot and tofu salad)
Tamatar or Mooli Chutney (Tomato or radish chutney)
Tofu Burfi (Tofu cheese diamonds)

Meals for Special Occasions

(Two special meals.)

Dahi Baras (Soybean and mung dal patties in yogurt)
Khaman Dhokla (Spicy soy cake)
Soy Poori (Deep-fried whole-wheat soy bread)
Mixed-Vegetable Korma with Tofu
Bharwa Mirch (Stuffed bell peppers with tofu)
Bundi and Soy-Yogurt Raita (Soy flour pearls raita)
Matar Paneer Pulav (Rice with peas and tofu)
Kakri Tofu Salad

Tofu Samosas (Pastry stuffed with tofu and potatoes)
Baati (Baked soy and whole-wheat flour balls)
Bharwa Kakri (Stuffed cucumbers with tofu)
Patta Gobhi Sabji (Cabbage with tofu)
Palak Tofu Salad (Spinach and tofu salad)
Dhania Tofu Chutney (Coriander tofu chutney)
Rice with Soy Okra
Toovar Dal with Soy Dal (Dried Pigeon peas with soy lentils)
Laddu (Sweet soy flour balls)

Weights, Measures, Temperatures and Times

Weights

As taste and eating habits vary, similarly cooking methods for the same recipe can be very different. A recipe is usually a guiding stick and depending on one's taste there is considerable room for creativity and intuition. The recipes in this book have accurate measurements and temperature settings. As one knows from experience, these are only recommended proportions and after some trial and error you can easily "tweek" the ingredients and cooking style to suit your family. Often in this book we have mentioned "according to taste"; these guidelines are meant to encourage you to experiment.

Weight measurements are given in the recipes. A novice should take the time to weigh the ingredients to insure consistent taste and quality in a particular dish. However, a seasoned cook can usually eyeball the weight. For dishes which will be cooked frequently, we have measured the ingredients by cups and spoons rather than weight.

A few simple precautions should be taken, however, when measuring with cups and spoons:

1. Fill the cup with dry ingredients and pass the edge of a knife over the top to level off.
2. When measuring the sifted flour, do not pack the cup tightly.
3. Melt the fat and then measure it.
4. When measuring tofu, cup should not be packed tightly. Fill with tofu and press lightly by hand.
5. Vegetables and other ingredients should not be packed tightly, just press very lightly by hand.

3 Teaspoons	=	1 Tablespoon	½ Pound sugar	=	1 Cup
4 Tablespoons	=	¼ Cup	16 Ounces	=	1 Pound or 1 pint
5⅓ Tablespoons	=	⅓ Cup	1 Ounce	=	2 Tablespoons
16 Tablespoons	=	1 Cup	1 Ounce	=	28 Grams
1 Cup	=	½ Pint	1 Pound	=	454 Grams
1 Cup	=	8 Fluid ounces	2.2 Pounds	=	1 Kilogram
2 Cups	=	1 Pint	1 Teaspoon	=	5 Milliliters (ml.)
4 Cups	=	1 Quart	1 Tablespoon	=	15 Ml.
4 Quarts	=	1 Gallon	1 Ounce (2 Tbsp.)	=	30 Ml.
8 Quarts	=	1 Peck	1 Cup	=	240 Ml.
4 Pecks	=	1 Bushel	1 Quart	=	950 Ml.
½ Pound margarine	=	1 Cup	1 Gallon	=	3800 Ml.
¼ Pound flour	=	1 Scant cup			

U.S. Standard Measures Equivalents
Approximate Metric Equivalents

Teacup: Measure full to the brim. The average American teacup, which is the one used in this book, is about 8 fluid ounces (240 ml.). An Indian teacup is about 7 fluid ounces (210 ml.). Adjustments should be made if using small size teacups.

Teaspoon: For liquids, measure full to the brim. For solids, use a heaped spoon. In terms of volume a teaspoon is approximately ⅙ fluid ounce (5 ml.).

Tablespoon: Measure same as for teaspoon. In terms of volume a tablespoon is about ½ fluid ounce (15 ml.) or approximately equal to 3 teaspoons.

Temperatures

The recipes state slow, medium, low medium or high medium heat. The approximate range for the oven temperature is given below in Fahrenheit and Centigrade.

The actual instructions of the oven manufacturer should be referred to for further guidance. Also, depending on the number of servings and relative proportions of ingredients, some additional temperature adjustments may need to be made.

Recipes	Approximate Oven Temperature F	C
Slow	250–300	121–149
Moderate	325–375	163–190
Hot	400–450	204–233
Very hot	475–500	246–260

Recipe Preparation Time

The time for cutting vegetables, soaking and freezing are not included in the recipe preparation time. The total time to prepare a recipe depends greatly on one's familiarity with the cooking process, mixing of the ingredients, and the ability to carry on multiple tasks.

Glossary of Hindi Terms

Hindi Names	English Meanings of Names
Aata	Whole-wheat flour
Adrak	Ginger root
Ajwain	Ajowan or carom seeds
Aloo	Potato
Amchoor	Mango powder
Baati	Baked whole-wheat flour balls
Badam	Almond
Bafala	Boiled and baked flour balls
Balu shahi	Sugar-coated doughnuts
Baingan	Eggplant
Basmati rice	Superior long grain rice
Bhatura	Fried flour bread
Besan	Chick-pea flour
Bhindi	Okra
Bundi	Soy or chick-pea flour pearls
Burfi	Sweet cheese diamonds
Chana dal	Split chick-pea
Channa	Fresh cheese
Chappati	Griddle-baked flat bread
Chaval	Rice
Chola	Chick-peas
Chilla	Thin pancake
Chutney	Relish made from spices
Dal chinne	Cinnamon
Corn dhokla	Boiled and baked corn balls
Dahi	Yogurt
Dahi baras	Patties in yogurt
Dal	Lentil or split pulse
Dalia	Cracked wheat
Dhania	Coriander
Doodh	Milk
Dosa	Rice pancakes
Gajar	Carrot
Garam masala	Powdered spices
Ghee	Clarified unsalted butter
Gobhi	Cauliflower
Gunja	Stuffed sweet pastry

Hindi Names	English Meanings of Names
Haldi	Turmeric
Halva	Sweet Pudding
Handvo	Pulse cake
Hara dhania	Fresh coriander
Hing	Asafetida
Hot mirch	Hot chilies
Idli	Steamed rice muffin
Imli	Tamarind
Jeera	Cumin seeds
Katcha	Raw
Kachori	Stuffed spicy pastry
Kaju	Cashew nut
Kalakand	Sweet pudding
Kakri	Cucumber
Kali mirch	Black pepper
Kala namak	Black salt
Kela	Banana
Kalonji	Nigella seeds
Keri	Unripe mango
Karela	Bitter melon, bitter gourd
Karhi patta	Curry leaves
Katcha tamatar	Unripe tomatoes
Khatta mitha	Sweet 'n' sour
Kesar	Saffron
Khaman dhokla	Steam cake
Khas-khas	White poppy seeds
Kheer	Pudding
Khopra	Dried coconut
Kishmish	Raisin
Khichadi	Rice with lentils
Kofta	Deep-fried vegetable balls
Korma	Preparation in thick sauce
Laddu	Sweet flour balls
Lal mirch	Red pepper
Lassi	Yogurt drink
Louki	Zucchini or bottle gourd
Maida	All-purpose flour
Malpua	Deep-fried pancakes in syrup
Matar	Peas
Mathari	Crunchies
Methi	Fenugreek
Micci bread	Spicy bread
Mirch	Capsicum or bell pepper
Mooli	White radish
Mooli pattha	Radish leaves
Moong dal	Dried mung pulse

Hindi Names	English Meanings of Names
Maisoor pak	Chick-pea and soy flour fudge
Naan	Crisp puffed bread
Naan khatai	Soft cookies
Namkin baati	Spicy baked flour balls
Namkin shakerpera	Spicy crunchies
Neem	Margosa tree leaves
Pakoras	Fritters
Palak	Spinach
Paneer	Pressed chenna cheese (or ricotta cheese)
Paratha	Fried bread
Patta	Leaves
Patta gobhi	Cabbage
Pista	Pistachio
Pitorh	Gram flour rolls
Podina	Mint
Poori	Deep-fried bread
Poran poli	Sweet stuffed bread
Pulav	Rice pilaf
Pyaz	Onion
Rai	Black mustard seeds
Raita	Seasoned yogurt salad
Roti	Griddle-baked flat bread
Sabji	Cooked spicy vegetables
Saive	Savory noodles
Sambar	Spicy vegetable and lentil stew
Sambar masala	Spices blended for sambar
Samosas	Stuffed potato pastry
Sandesh	Fresh cheese pudding
Sevaiyan	Vermicelli
Shakerpera	Diamond shape crunchies
Shrikhand	Yogurt pudding
Tamatar	Tomatoes
Tej patta	Cassia leaf
Thandai	Spicy drink
Ticci	Patties
Til	Sesame seeds
Toovar dal	Dried pigeon split pea lentils
Urad dal	Black gram lentils without skin
Vegetable pakoras	Vegetable fritters

APPENDIX D

Sources of Indian Foods

You may find many of the ingredients for recipes in this book at your health food store, specialty food store, or some markets, but you may need also to consult some of the following sources, listed alphabetically by state.

International Food
5054 E McDowell Road
Phoenix, AZ 85008
Tel: (602)273-6777

Ganesh Grocery
2633 W Lincoln Avenue
Anaheim, CA 92801
Tel: (714)952-0542

Bombay Grocery
2703 W Lincoln Avenue
Anaheim, CA 92801
Tel: (714)761-3871

Bombay Spices
18628 Pioneer Blvd.
Artesia, CA 90701
Tel: (213)860-9949

Patel Brothers
18636 S Pioneer Blvd
Artesia, CA 90701
Tel: (213)402-2953

House of Spices
8440-A Kass Drive
Buena Park, CA 90621
Tel: (714)739-1455

Asian Gifts & Groceries
1690 W 6th Street
Corona, CA 91720
Tel: (714)736-8612

Ganesh Groceries, Inc.
303-2 Dimondbar Blvd.
Dimondbar, CA 91765
Tel: (714)860-3968

India Spices
3931 Washington Blvd.
Fremont, CA 94538
Tel: (415)657-4965

Amar Deep
39110 State Street
Fremont, CA 94538
Tel: (415)794-6747

Houses of Spices
12223 E Centralia Street
Lakewood, CA 90715
Tel: (213)860-9919

India Bazar
11415 W Washington Blvd.
Los Angeles, CA 90066
Tel: (213)313-3228

Indian Spices & Grocery
5891 W Pico Blvd.
Los Angeles, CA 90019
Tel: (213)931-4871

Apna Bazar
1239½ S Fairfax Avenue
Los Angeles, CA 90019
Tel: (213)932-2762

India Spices
17020 Devonshire Street
Northridge, CA 91325
Tel: (818)366-3662

Patel Brothers
8516 Reseda Blvd. Unit 8
Northridge, CA 91324
Tel: (818)772-7691

Asia Mart
19151 E Colima Road
Rowland Heights, CA 91748
Tel: (213)965-6255

India Spice & Gift Bazaar
3060 Clairemont Drive
San Diego, CA 92117
Tel: (619)276-7226

India Gifts & Food
643 Post Street
San Francisco, CA 94109
Tel: (415)771-5041

International Food Bazaar
2058 Curtner Avenue
San Jose, CA 95124
Tel: (408)559-3397

Apna Spiceland
2707 Thousand Oaks Blvd.
Thousand Oaks, CA 91360
Tel: (805)373-6761

Asia Spices
2776 W Sepulveda Blvd.
Torrance, CA 90505
Tel: (213)530-4634

Raja Gifts & Grocery
14445 Newport Avenue
Tustin, CA 92680
Tel: (714)669-1104

Dana Bazaar
193 Shunpike Road
Cromwell, CT 06416
Tel: (203)635-0502

Stepstone Hill Market
350 Stepstone Hill Road
Guilford, CT 06437
Tel: (203)453-5023

Patel Brothers, Inc.
1870 West 60th Street
Hialeah, FL 33012
Tel: (305)557-5536

House of Spices
107 O'Leary Drive
Bensenville, IL
Tel: (312)595-2929

India Gifts & Foods
1031 W Belmont Avenue
Chicago, IL 60657
Tel: (312)348-4393

Apna Bazaar
2314 W Devon Avenue
Chicago, IL 60659
Tel: (312)262-4200

Patel Brothers
2610 W Devon Avenue
Chicago, IL 60659
Tel: (312)262-7777

Indian Tea and Spices
453 Common Street
Belmont, MA 02178
Tel: (617)484-3737

Framingham India Grocery
199 Concord Street
Framingham, MA 07101
Tel: (508)872-6120

Sangam House
482 Moody Street
Waltham, MA 02154
Tel: (617)484-3500

Patel Brothers, Inc.
2080 University Blvd.
Langley Park, MD 20783
Tel: (301)422-1555

J & V International
1275 Bloomfield Avenue Suite 7
Fairfield, NJ 07006
Tel: (201)575-9575

Bombay Bazaar
781 Newark Avenue
Jersey City, NJ 07306
Tel: (201)963-5907

Gandhi Grocers, Inc.
773 Newark Avenue
Jersey City, NJ 07306
Tel: (201)792-4794

Asia Bazaar
520 Ernston Road
Parlin, NJ 08859
Tel: (201)727-0916

India Seasons
5012 S Arville Street
Las Vegas, NV 89118
Tel: (702)876-0822

India Food & Spices
3661 S Maryland Parkway
Las Vegas, NV 89109
Tel: (702)733-0640

Taj Mahal
Indo Pak Grocery
120 Coniland
Brooklyn, NY 11230
Tel: (718)859-6346

Indian Groceries & Spices, Inc.
61 Wythe Avenue
Brooklyn, NY 11211
Tel: (718)963-0177

Anna Bhandar
82-80 Broadway
Elmhurst, NY 11373
Tel: (718)478-6912

Kalustyan's
123 Lexington Avenue
New York, NY 10016
Tel: (212)685-3451

Little India Stores, Inc.
128 E 28th Street
New York, NY 10016
Tel: (212)683-1691

Indian Spice World, Inc.
126 Lexington Avenue
New York, NY 10016
Tel: (212)686-2727

House of Spices
4605 N 6th Street
Philadelphia, PA 19140
Tel: (215)455-6870

Home Fair
3253 Old Frankstown Road
Pittsburg, PA 15239
Tel: (412)325-4343

Bombay Emporium
294 Craft Avenue
Pittsburgh, PA 15213
Tel: (412)682-4965

International Bazaar
3936 Monroeville Blvd.
Monroeville, PA 15146
Tel: (412)373-7171

House of Spices, Inc.
13929 N Central Expwy Suite 419
Dallas, TX 75243
Tel: (214)783-7544

Bombay Imports
2301 N O'Connor Suite 1
Irving, TX 75060
Tel: (214)255-3037

Quicks Food Mart
89-D Street 2nd Avenue
Salt Lake City, UT 84103
Tel: (801)531-1652

Reddy's International
15600 N.E. 8th Street Blvd.
Bellevue, WA 98008
Tel: (206)643-4263

Biographical Notes

Laxmi Jain, a native of India, has lived in the Boston area for the past 18 years. She works actively to promote the use of soybeans in the American and Indian diet. Mrs. Jain has developed original recipes which have been published in local newspapers in both the U.S.A. and India. Her first book on soybean, "Indian Soy Cuisine," was published by the American Soybean Association. She has also lectured and given demonstrations at various schools and health promotion organizations.

Dr. Manoj Jain is a physician in Internal Medicine at Boston City Hospital and is specializing in International Health and Infectious Diseases at the New England Medical Center. Dr. Jain is a graduate of Boston University School of Engineering, School of Medicine and School of Public Health. He received a Medical Perspectives fellowship to research the uses of soy foods in the Indian diet, and has published his results in the medical literature. Dr. Jain has conducted talk shows and soy demonstrations on national television and radio in India. Currently, Dr. Jain is also a consultant in a five-year rural health and soybean promotion project in India. With his mother, Mrs. Laxmi Jain, Dr. Jain has developed numerous recipes with the maximum nutritional content.